MW01088187

LIFE IS A LAZY SUSAN OF SH*T SANDWICHES

LIFE IS A LAZY SUSAN OF SH*T SANDWICHES

JENNIFER WELCH AND ANGIE SULLIVAN

HANOVER
SQUARE
PRESS

HANOVER
SQUARE
PRESS™

Recycling programs
for this product may
not exist in your area.

ISBN-13: 978-1-335-55098-9

Life Is a Lazy Susan of Sh*t Sandwiches

Copyright © 2025 by I've Had It With Jen & Pumps, LLC

All rights reserved. No part of this book may be used or reproduced in any manner whatsoever without written permission.

Without limiting the author's and publisher's exclusive rights, any unauthorized use of this publication to train generative artificial intelligence (AI) technologies is expressly prohibited.

This publication contains opinions and ideas of the author. It is intended for informational and educational purposes only. The reader should seek the services of a competent professional for expert assistance or professional advice. Reference to any organization, publication or website does not constitute or imply an endorsement by the author or the publisher. The author and the publisher specifically disclaim any and all liability arising directly or indirectly from the use or application of any information contained in this publication.

TM and ® are trademarks of Harlequin Enterprises ULC.

Hanover Square Press
22 Adelaide St. West, 41st Floor
Toronto, Ontario M5H 4E3, Canada
HanoverSqPress.com

Printed in U.S.A.

For Javi
In a world full of shit sandwiches, you were always warm and golden.

CONTENTS

LIFE IS A LAZY SUSAN OF SH*T SANDWICHES

INTRODUCTION: LIFE IS A LAZY SUSAN OF SHIT SANDWICHES

JEN

STANDING BACKSTAGE AT THE Variety Playhouse, I almost shat myself. Not from digestive issues, since I have an iron stomach, but as I peered through the curtain at the audience of our first live, sold-out show and saw all those good citizens of Atlanta, Georgia, I wondered why the darn beta-blocker still hadn't kicked in. That pill was supposed to lower my heart rate, but I had so much adrenaline coursing through my body that ten of those things probably wouldn't have done a damn thing.

Meanwhile, my best friend and co-podcaster Angie "Pumps" Sullivan clutched a stack of index cards and hyperventilated. Her black dress—bought on sale from Amazon, where Pumps did most of her shopping—in stark contrast to her signature matte red lip. As I watched her flip through our talking points, wild-eyed, like a possum in a trap, it struck me: not just how far we'd come but how remarkable it was that anyone wanted to hear the two of us talk about ourselves and our journey, an overused word we both loathed but one that fitted the current occasion to a T.

"I can't believe that so many people want to hear us bitch and complain," Pumps said, grabbing my hand and giving it a bone-crushing squeeze. "Are they nuts? Are we nuts? Also, that fucking beta-blocker isn't doing shit."

The raw physicality of the gesture brought a lump to my throat. Although Pumps is a hugger, we aren't necessarily touchy-feely types. Still, the gravity of the current situation warranted some handholding, evidenced by the strength of Pumps's squeeze. I knew that hand so well. For the past twenty years, I'd watched it soothe babies and push strollers. I'd seen it hold cigarettes, wineglasses, and imitation designer handbags. I'd seen it apply foundation with a sponge and wipe it off with a facecloth. I'd observed it furiously typing on an iPad and clutching the steering wheel of her Audi as she turned onto the freeway. I knew that hand, face, and voice as well as my own, if not better.

Pumps is my closest friend. The one who has been there for me through it all, the good, the bad, and the ugly. That's why I agreed to write the introduction to this book. Not because I drew the short straw or I'm codependent (well, more on that later, a whole lot more), but because Pumps *asked* me to do it. There are only four people in the world I would do anything for. Two of those people came out of my vagina, one is my mother, and the other is Pumps. When our listeners write in to ask if my husband (Josh), Pumps, and I are in a throuple, we joke that we are, but the real answer is no—that would mean way too much sex and too many date nights. Too much processing.

But if it weren't for our friendship, I'm not sure Pumps would be alive, or I'd still be married. I don't know if she'd be sober or if I'd be a budding racquet-sports sensation. And before you worry about my marriage, yes, Josh also supports me emotionally. Yes, he's a great guy who still has hair like early-career George Clooney. But when things go apeshit-bananas, Pumps is my phone call. My partner in crime. My rudder in the storm.

If there's one thing I've learned from my years on this planet, American culture has unrealistic expectations about happiness and balance. We live in a fractured society in which social media filters and AI create a false front. Everyone looks happy, perfect, smooth, and forever young with something the internet calls "glass skin." The messages we internalize, that we should be hotter, richer, more fulfilled, only increase our feelings of inadequacy. The relentless drive toward well-ness counterproductively serves to make us feel unwell. The search for total happiness leads to unhappiness. The quest for total balance leads to imbalance.

You know that game people play when everyone goes around the table saying what they would do if they won Powerball for a gazillion dollars? I hate to break this to you, but even if you won the lottery and paid off all your student loans, your car, and your mortgage, then went on an all-expenses-paid vacation to the Maldives, you might only be happy for a nanosecond before a whole host of other problems cropped up. You'd be in one of those thatched huts over the turquoise waters of the Indian Ocean thinking, *I want to be on a yacht in Bora Bora.* As soon as you attained that *one thing* you thought you had to have or die trying, your mind would create a new void with other unattainable wants and desires. Because that's how the human mind functions. It wants more, more, more. The latest designer handbag, a bigger house, and the latest iPhone. Hotter sex. New clothes. Different spouse. Different lips. Different face.

But so many things in life are out of our control: We get crow's feet. Our parents get old and die. Our children grow from sweet, sweet babies who hide behind our shins and call out for us at night to teenagers who answer k when we text I love you. Adulthood is the ultimate bait and switch. Our dream jobs turn out to be staring at spreadsheets and answering endless passive-aggressive emails or attending Zoom meetings that could have been emails. The bills, disappointments, and crushed expectations rain down on us like a monsoon.

When I was growing up in South Oklahoma City, my mother had a lazy Susan—a rotating circular device that holds food, spices, and condiments—in the kitchen cabinet. Lazy Susans are famously prevalent in Chinese restaurants where food is set on a turntable and served family style. Some people think Thomas Jefferson brought the concept of the lazy Susan to America from France or "invented it" for his daughter Susan, who complained that she was always last at the dinner table to get her chicken and gravy. Some say the name comes from the eighteenth-century moniker for servants, called "Susans." I used to picture adult life as a lazy Susan, a rotating smorgasbord of options and choices, nothing fancy, just something fun and easier to handle and digest.

I don't know why I thought this; my parents never modeled a perfect marriage—my dad, like many men of his generation, most likely had untreated PTSD from his tour in Vietnam. He could be angry and withdrawn, and my mother never found her footing in an intellectually fulfilling career—but they seemed happy enough. My mom read voraciously, and my dad raised racing pigeons in the backyard. On TV, I saw a lot of mothers who smiled as they joyfully slid pot roasts in and out of the oven. Every show seemed to depict couples who modeled breezy conjugal contentment. I don't know what I thought marriage was supposed to be. Was it Mike and Carol Brady? The kooky antics of Lucy and Ricky? My parents rarely drank, yet somehow, Angie and I both married lawyers who turned out to be married to drugs and alcohol and, in Angie's case, sex workers. No matter how I spun it, my life became a lazy Susan of shit sandwiches. The wheel turned and turned, and I always got a grilled turd.

When things got especially grim for me and Josh, when he was in the absolute throes of his addiction and I was at my most bereft, I spent a lot of time fantasizing about having normal-people problems. Pumps and I have talked about this desire a lot. How we wished that our biggest problem was being bored in our marriages or annoyed by some petty, quotidian concern. Sometimes, at lunch with a friend, I found myself struck dumb when that friend's biggest grievance was "my husband's messy," or "he doesn't load dishes in the dishwasher the way I like," or simply, "he snores."

In those moments, I had nothing to add. I couldn't tell those very well-meaning people, "My husband hits the bar like it's the Lightning Lane at Disney World."

Anyone who knows me more than five minutes knows I don't love Disney World. It's too crowded and it's almost impossible to get a decent salad. When my kids were young, I took them there on more than one occasion. I dutifully rode Pirates of the Caribbean, and It's a Small World. I ate the giant turkey leg. Would I have rather been at the Ritz in Paris, wearing a peach robe and eating a gorgeous room service breakfast? Yes. But I did genuinely enjoy myself. My kids were happy, so I was happy. That said, as an adult, I would never say to Pumps, "Hey, we're in LA without the kids. Do you want to go to Disney, just me and you, two grown-ass women?" Maybe I'm a coldhearted, horrible person, but I also don't understand why these Disney adults would want to get married at the Magic Kingdom or have Mickey and Goofy in their bridal party.

Look, life is hard. Being human can sometimes suck. No new news. The great thinkers have been writing about the suckiness of life since writing was invented. But, as long as you aren't joining the NRA, do whatever you have to do to make it through the day, Mackensleigh. Put on those Mickey Mouse ears and spend your whole paycheck on Buzz Lightyear merch and soggy pizza. If that's your strategy for navigating adversity, go for it. Desperate times call for desperate treasures.

Life may well be suffering but here's the catch: We don't have to suffer alone. In fact, guess what? We can *bond* over our suffering.

If Pumps and I have learned anything—and we haven't learned much, that's why this book is so short—it's that we need friends who can laugh with us through the pain. Humor can get us through just about everything. We can laugh at helicopter parents and people who say "*We're* pregnant" instead of "I'm pregnant." We can bond over the things we can't stand, like Stanley cups and MAGA Republicans. Nothing is a greater palate cleanser than a good bitch session.

We wanted to write this book because we made it. Not to this live show or behind a podcast mic, but because we made it here, to this moment, in one piece, together. Angie and I joke all the time about how something is deeply wrong with us because we laughed at so many of the bad things that happened to us, things that would have leveled a lot of people. We are forever entertained and amazed by the royal shit show of our own lives. And *that*, we've realized, is the whole point.

"Let's hear it for Jennifer Welch and Angie Sullivan!" boomed the familiar voice of our producer, followed by cheering and thunderous applause. My heart beat a mean mambo in my chest. If there were a bucket nearby, I probably would have leaned over and puked right into it.

"This is it," I said. "I love you, Pumps." Pumps nodded, her platinum hair backlit like an angel on a Christmas tree in a Lifetime movie. She glanced at me, then peeked through a small crack in the curtain.

"I love you too," she said, squeezing my hand so hard my wedding ring almost fractured my pinky. "I can't believe all these fucking people came here to see us."

"This is as bad as it's ever going to be," I said. "Every show after this will be easier." Pumps looked again through the gap in the curtain and then back at me. Right away, we returned to our usual mind meld. It was as if I could see both of our thoughts synchronously projected onto the curtain like an old-fashioned newsreel. We were thinking about how we'd been to hell and back together. We were thinking it could not be possible that all these people—in this sold-out show— were coming to see us. And then, we did what we always do; we took one look at each other and busted a gut. Laughing and misty-eyed, I cursed myself for not bringing a tissue— until Pumps pulled one out of nowhere and handed it to me. If I had a higher power, I would have thanked them. Instead, I thanked Pumps and walked onto the stage.

D) ALL OF THE ABOVE

~~~~~~~~

ANGIE

I WAS RAISED TO believe Jesus was my best friend. It's hard to say who introduced Jesus and me. My mother, or maybe her mother or her mother before her. Though maybe in Oklahoma, you're just born with this familiarity, the way you can tell if a tornado's coming from the color of the sky. Until I met Jennifer, I didn't know a single person who was an atheist. Of course, intellectually, I knew atheists existed, like I knew there were Hollywood celebrities, but just like I never bumped into Julia Roberts or Nicole Kidman at the supermarket, I never encountered any atheists in my daily life. I didn't start poking holes in my belief system until 2019 when my biological father died, and I quit going to church. But I'm getting ahead of myself.

I met Jennifer through her husband, Josh. He and I were both attorneys and knew each other through legal circles. I was chatting with him one day about the tired decor I had going in my house, and he suggested hiring his wife, Jennifer, to help me with a redesign. Here's the thing: I have zero taste. When I say zero, I mean zero. I told Jen as much on her very first walk-through. I don't like museums or the theater. I don't like art. I don't have signs from Michael's that say *Wine O'clock*, or *This Kitchen Is for Dancing*, but if someone were to buy me one, I might just find a spot to hang it up. So, I really needed an interior designer.

When Jen got a load of my dining room, her face scrunched up like she swallowed a wasp.

"The only thing worse than silk flowers is a painting of silk flowers," she told me. "And you have both."

You'd think I'd be offended, but I fucking loved it. I started laughing and the two of us bonded immediately. Jen was outspoken and unapologetic, and I admired that, even though our upbringings were diametrically opposed.

Jennifer was raised secular, and I went to Sunday school and church on Sundays. In high school, I was homecoming queen, and all-American cheerleader. Everything in my early life had a religious undertone. My family attended an Evangelical megachurch, the kind where they sing Christian hymns, and the preacher delivers hellfire-and-damnation sermons about Jesus. These sermons were designed to terrify us into being good Christians and to control our behavior when we weren't in church. I grew up in purity culture, which promulgates the idea of sexual abstinence. It meant girls didn't wear skimpy clothes or stay out late, doing things like teenage drinking or anything that might threaten their precious virginity, including dating. I didn't wear a purity ring, but I certainly didn't have sex or run around with "bad kids."

My mother grew up this way and her mother before her. You know how if you're on a diet, there's something called a "cheat day," when you can go crazy and eat all the junk food you want? Well, in purity culture, at least where I was concerned, there were maybe a few workarounds, but there was no "cheating." You were in or you were out. Pure or impure. And I didn't question it. At least, not initially.

My parents were from Muskogee, Oklahoma, a city of about thirty-eight thousand people made famous by the Merle Haggard song, "Okie from Muskogee." They weren't backward but they also weren't cosmopolitan by any stretch. My mother taught me how to make pot roast and flaky, buttery biscuits. She worked hard and helped me to see the good in people even when I couldn't see it in myself. She also adhered strictly to her faith and never questioned the status quo. Her faith was as comforting as a chain restaurant in a strange city; you always knew what would be on the menu and how it would taste.

My stepdad always said, "There's nothing good girls need to be a part of after 11:30 p.m." He came home every night at six so we could eat family dinner together. He rarely drank. He asked me questions about school or cheerleading practice, even when I could see he was tired from being on his feet all day at my parents' convenience store. After dinner, we all watched *Matlock* or *Murder, She Wrote*. But mostly, I went upstairs and did my homework to the familiar sounds of my parents watching TBN or GOD TV downstairs.

That's why my husband Kirk's sex addiction utterly baffled me. I'd never encountered anything like it. Yes, I'd seen *Law*

and Order SVU and *Fatal Attraction*. I'd read *Othello*. My mom
and dad had gotten divorced when I was three, but I could
barely remember them as married. I knew affairs occurred,
but the idea seemed abstract. In the real world, I believed,
good, Christian people didn't stray from their marriages.
They just did what they were supposed to do; they worked
and came home to say grace and eat their chicken and gravy
then put on their pajamas, like my stepdad. They didn't bang
enough sex workers to fill every seat in the Paycom Center.

Even though Kirk's proclivities shocked them, my parents
were there for me when my world got rocked to its core. Then
they were there for me when I went to rehab for painkill-
ers. Kirk eventually lost our house and we ended up getting divorced. My parents put a down payment on a small
place for me and the kids to live in, so we could start over.
I returned to work as a divorce lawyer, a career I'd given up
when I became a mother. Sitting in the shock of it all, unable
to comprehend the loss, I despaired that I would never feel
like myself again. Like any supposedly devout Christian, I
looked for signs and symbols everywhere: pop songs, people,
menus, and literal signs on the freeway. Wasn't Jesus supposed
to protect me from all this crap? Had he been on a coffee
break when Kirk cheated? I'd done all the things I was supposed to do. I'd prayed and sang and supposedly believed. I'd
come home right after cheerleading practice and done all my
homework and my chores. I was polite and I went to Bible
study. What in the Sam Hill happened?

Before I got sober, I would call Jennifer, and she'd answer
on the first ring like she'd sensed my need in the ether. I'd say,

"Let's burn," which was our code for "Let's smoke cigarettes on our respective porches and talk about all the shenanigans our husbands have got themselves up to." And by "our husbands," I mostly meant mine, although her husband, Josh, had his own struggles with addiction. Jen and I understood each other on a visceral level.

As soon as we met, we started communicating incessantly. It wasn't just that we got along; my mind couldn't accept blank space. Silence scared the bejesus out of me. More than anything, I needed something to hold on to. A sounding board or some sort of ballast. Maybe this was why, years later, when I went to rehab, I clung to the people there like my own kin. I felt like I was on a raft with them, floating in the middle of chum-filled, shark-infested waters.

The only problem was when people would look around the circle during those early twelve-step meetings and gush about their "higher power," it gave me the ick. It was weird because that kind of talk wasn't new to me, considering my Evangelical origins, but the whole God-as-my-savior thing had ceased to have the same pull. In other words, somewhere along the way, that argument stopped working for me. My biological father had died, and I started looking out to the larger world for answers. His death led me to deconstruct my faith, which is when Evangelicals question all the things they've been told not to question, like God wrote the Bible and you can turn anything into a salad, if you put enough mayonnaise on it. I started reading Freud and Copernicus. I stopped thinking that the Bible was the be all and end all. It occurred to me that the idea of ONE

BOOK containing *all the answers* was what got humans into trouble in the first place.

Yes, I grew up believing in a certain skinny thirty-three-year-old carpenter who died for my sins, and, yes, sometimes I questioned some of His decisions, like why were there so many wars in God's name? Why did kids get cancer? Why did I have to pay for Wi-Fi on flights when I'd already paid for an overpriced ticket? Why did Trump exist? How did I end up in a church basement, looking at slogans on a wall that read *One Day at a Time* and *Let Go or Be Dragged*. How were these signs any different from those signs at Michael's? *Bless This Mess! Home Sweet Home! Dogs Welcome, People Tolerated!*

But the truth was, after my dad died, I just couldn't get it up for God in the same way anymore. I couldn't conjure the faith or the feeling. Look, a lot is fuzzy from those first months of early sobriety, but I can remember Jennifer calling me when I first got to rehab, her voice thick with compassion and worry.

"Angie," she said. "If you need to reconnect with your faith, I want you to know I support you. Do whatever you need to do to get sober." As she spoke, I looked at a poster of a Matisse coastal scene on the wall, the kind that is ubiquitous in schools and hospitals.

"Please," I said. "Just because I have a drug problem doesn't mean I believe that nonsense," I told her.

Later that night, I considered dropping to my knees by the side of the bed. The Eleventh Step encourages us to seek solace through prayer and meditation, and I was raised to be a good girl, to follow the rules. I'd taught Bible studies! Logged countless hours singing my heart out in church. I'd previously believed that if I did all the right things, I'd be rewarded in this life and the next. Now, I was supposed to follow the program of Alcoholics Anonymous, whose founder, Bill Wilson, was influenced by none other than—you guessed it—the Evangelical movement.

Still, I couldn't bring myself to get on my knees and pray that night. It felt performative. It felt like a lie. And I was done lying—to myself and everyone else.

I began to reframe my thinking. My first AA sponsor made it abundantly clear that *anything* could be my higher power, even a group of recovering addicts with coffee breath, dandruff, and unwashed hair. Sitting in church basements for Narcotics Anonymous or AA meetings, I could feel the power of the collective swell around me. A nice, healing group of gal pals I could get behind. This sensation, I realized, was as familiar to me as my mother's voice in church singing "He Is Our Peace." The goal was the same—to step outside myself for a minute and remember that I was part of a larger whole.

Growing up, I did not have this perspective. Instead, my relationship with a higher power was rooted in fear and shame. If I did more than make out with a boy, I felt guilty and confused. I knew I wanted to kiss boys but also that I shouldn't want to kiss them. So, I tamped down all my sexual urges. I put so much pressure on myself to be the perfect Bible-Belt girl, then the perfect wife and mother, that I couldn't even see the ways in which my life was falling apart. How had I ended up where I did? In part, because I stayed attached to the rules of my religion when I really should've been giving more credence to the tiny, holy acts that occur on any given day. A Beyoncé song while I'm driving. A really great strawberry milkshake at Braum's Ice Cream & Dairy. Watching my mother brine brisket in the kitchen—that was, in its way, a kind of offering.

I've had it with Evangelicals. I've had it with purity culture. I've had it with the haters, the pro-lifers, and homophobes. After I began to question my belief system, I learned that Christianity became the prevailing religion in antiquity in part because it promised an utopic afterlife, especially if you followed the instruction manual. But in 2019, I stopped believing in an afterlife. I stopped believing in the manual. I stopped believing that some spirit in a beard and a nightgown would save me and take me to heaven. I can't say what I believe in anymore, except Rachel Maddow. Does this terrify me sometimes? Yes. Do I feel free? Also, yes. The tide goes in, the tide goes out. Let it come. Let it go. Let it be.

THE RAPTURE

~~~~~~~~~~

JEN

AS A DYED-IN-THE-WOOL DEMOCRAT in a red state, I find myself in a lot of social situations in which I'm surrounded by deeply Christian, deeply red Republicans who are sounding off on topics like socialized health care or gay marriage. I've learned that if you don't speak up in a red state, rights get taken away. If you give these politicians an inch, they keep moving the goalposts further and further until the next thing you know, abortion is illegal and you're living in *The Handmaid's Tale*.

Funnily enough, when I first met Pumps, I assumed she was a Christian Republican. This wasn't that wild of an assumption; 79 percent of the population of Oklahoma is Christian and 47 percent is Evangelical. So, it was what it was. I don't believe in magical thinking. I think there's only this life, and that life's temporariness lends it beauty and pathos. I don't know what happens next. Whatever we bring to this earth is our gift and this gift is finite. Yet somehow, standing in Pumps's dining room for the first time, I felt like I'd known her forever and she'd known me.

I was surprised to feel an immediate kinship with Angie, considering her Christian beliefs and her deeply ingrained Republicanism. These points of view would ultimately shift, but when we first met, they lurked around the edges of our friendship like a bat in the rafters.

My difficulty with these leanings goes back to early childhood. My peers, who I suppose meant well, would constantly bludgeon me for my supposed spiritual deficits. When I was in third grade, a friend merrily told me all about Satan: how, in the afterlife, my skin would burn off, then grow back, only to burn off again. Demons would surround me and poke my eyes out, which would also grow back only to be gouged out and grow back yet again. And this jolly process would continue forever. Why would anyone ascribe to this belief system or worship a God who would choose to inflict this kind of eternal punishment? It left me dumbfounded.

When I was in the eighth grade I learned that Nostradamus had predicted the exact date and time of the Rapture, which was when the Messiah would return to earth, the believers would ascend to heaven and the sinners would be dragged to an eternity in hell. Weirdly enough—or luckily depending on your point of view—the exact moment of this event was due to occur during our eighth-grade football game. I heard all my fellow cheerleaders saying stuff like, "I could be in the middle of doing a toe touch and my pompoms will just fall to the ground." Or a football player would say, "I'll be running to the end zone and my uniform, and my football pads and the ball will melt away." And I just remember thinking, *This is fucking crazy.*

But these people were my peers, my social group. I wanted to fit in, so I just said, "I really don't think that's going to happen." But everyone around me worried constantly about spiritual warfare: everywhere they went, they believed demons and angels were waging a holy war over everything they said and did. If they made the right decision, the angels won. If they made the wrong decision, the demons won. They seemed so tortured about it.

Well, guess what? The big game came and went. Much to everyone's great surprise, not only did we win the game, but everybody left with their pompoms intact. The Rapture never came. Or, if it did, I didn't notice.

But time stood still the day I walked into Angie's dining room and saw her hideous decor. She was so attractive and full of life, with a megawatt personality and a great sense of humor. But she had this grandmotherly aesthetic that slapped you in the face as soon as you crossed her threshold. She also had piss-poor politics and believed God created the earth and rested on the seventh day, rather than the Big Bang having anything to do with it. Nevertheless, she still became my "Angelina Pumpkintina," the nickname Josh gave her, whence the moniker "Pumps" evolved and stuck.

"I have no taste," Pumps announced.

"Oh, I can tell," I said, and started mentally making over Angie's whole house. We were both in the same season of our lives—both married to attorneys. She had two kids and was pregnant with her third. I had my son Dylan. I wasn't yet pregnant with my second child, Roman, but it was in the cards. We all get influxes of friends at different times in our lives. I had my college friends, then my young-mom friends, the ones I saw all the time at the playground and the toddler music classes around town. Having young kids was isolating; I couldn't just up and go anywhere like I used to, so Angie and I bonded right away, even though we weren't totally compatible on paper.

Pumps drove this white Suburban I affectionately named the Petri Dish because there were always rogue Chicken Mc-Nuggets from McDonald's wedged into the seats. Every day, our husbands went to their respective law offices to spend the day with the adult populace, and then we got together, loading up the Petri Dish to take the kids to toddler gymnastics, or to the all-you-can-eat pizza buffet at Mazzio's, or to Chuck E. Cheese, any number of wretched places you have to go to when you have little kids. George W. Bush was president, a leader I didn't like or trust one iota. I remember early on in our friendship Pumps praised him and I told her I couldn't stand him. She looked at me like I told her I hated Santa. Then she asked me about "my faith," which was Oklahoma for "what church do you belong to and how loudly do you thump your Bible?"

"I'm a non-Christian," I said, which was my standard answer. Pumps's eyes flashed. I remember thinking how exhausting it was to exist as a rational thinker in the Bible Belt. No one judged you based on your character; instead it was all about how many times per week you went to church.

Pumps constantly brought up her faith. She even invited me to Bible study with her at least once a week. Finally, I said, "Look, I'm not going to your Bible study. I'm not trying to change your beliefs, and I wish you would stop meddling in mine." But the thing about Evangelicals is they get their biblical panties in a twist trying to save you. It practically makes them salivate. Pumps was relentless until I put up a hard boundary to get her to stop trying to recruit me, which meant we didn't have to toil ceaselessly over the supposedly sorry state of my soul. I was always thankful to her for that. It opened other avenues of discourse for things we both found despicable—like preschool graduations and soggy fried chicken. We found common ground complaining about cold queso, limp handshakes, and people who take too long with their drink order at Starbucks. *You always order the same drink, Ashlee! Just order your grande vanilla latte no whip and stop staring at the menu!* In a way, those rides in Petri Dish were the precursor to *I've Had It*. Two women, laughing and kvetching about every little thing under the sun. In the early days, except for certain no-fly zones—God and our voting records—we were completely simpatico. Angie understood on a visceral level what I was going through when I talked about Josh's early struggles. She empathized when I told her I wanted something I couldn't have and married the wrong man to get it. She got it. She got me.

As the world grows more fractured, I find it a real challenge to coexist amongst people who hold views that seem diametrically opposed to my own. I've struggled to see the humanity in anyone who would vote for a president who doesn't care about a woman's right to choose, doesn't want to protect trans kids or fund public libraries or protect our environment. I cannot tolerate or abide hatred of any kind. I believe that everyone deserves to be treated with dignity. I will die on that hill.

And yet . . . I know people can change. Angie did. I always knew there was more to Angie than her terrible politics. And I also believed that she could evolve. I saw her heart and her kindness. The purity culture of her youth had brainwashed her into seeing the world one way. When I say "world," I mean the heteronormative, Christian megachurch in Oklahoma. I still struggle to balance my compassion and empathy with the more pressing need for allyship and speaking up. There's no simple formula. But when people show you goodness, like Angie did, those positive aspects are worth embracing.

One day, Pumps and I were in the Petri Dish, driving up Nichols Road, when she said, "Did you know that human beings used to live to be nine hundred years old?" This was one of her conversation starters. Whenever she brought up the subject of her megachurch—wouldn't I like to join her one Sunday, an event that had about as much chance of happening as getting killed by a vending machine twice—she would bring up some deranged fact that sounded like something Tom Cruise would believe about Scientology.

"Angie," I said slowly, like I was talking to a toddler. "Girl. That never happened."

"Yes, it did," she said, a slight adolescent lilt to her voice. "I learned it in Bible study."

"This is objectively and verifiably false," I continued. "Modern man lives longer than ever before because of two things—filtered water and access to modern medications."

"But there was no disease in the Garden of Eden!" she chirped, a competent attorney who was nevertheless taking these age-old tales at face value. I argued that the Garden of Eden was yet another metaphor for how people are always striving to attain something unattainably perfect, a womb-state from which they feel they have been exiled, and we went back and forth about subjective intent versus scientific truth. None of these conversations were adversarial in nature; it was clear that we came from completely different worlds, and I never feel like it's my job on this earth to reverse-proselytize a more sensible way of thinking to Evangelicals.

When my son Dylan and Angie's daughter, Emily, were thirteen years old, Emily told Dylan she'd learned in school that humans didn't evolve from apes. "Evolution wasn't a *thing*." Meanwhile, Dylan had learned about Charles Darwin. He later asked me how Angie could send Emily to a school where people learned these things. Of course, what I wanted to say was, "Fuck if I know why that crazy Bible-beater sends her daughter there." Instead, I explained to Dylan that Fundamentalism discourages critical thinking and denies facts. I told him about how I think these schools indoctrinate children with fear, not to mention magical thinking. The world is a big place, and the more you open your mind to see the big picture, the good, the bad, and the ass-backward, the better you know yourself and your place in it.

In 2008, I threw all my chips in for Obama. I had an Obama sign on my lawn. I wore a pin. I had a HOPE T-shirt. An Obama portrait. I made the case to Pumps about the reasons I was voting for Obama: Withdrawing troops from Iraq, and the attempt to repeal DOMA, etc. I explained that I supported human rights and felt a moral calling to support marginalized groups. Initially, Pumps's worldview was "if it doesn't affect me, IDGAF," which sounds worse than it is, because she was so kind and loving, she just wasn't the staunch ally and advocate she would later become. So, I used her faith to convince her. I would say, "Don't you think Jesus would want poor people to have access to better education and housing? Don't you think he, a man who preached about people loving one another, would loathe racism?" Pumps had to agree. Yes, the Son of God would want good public schools. He wouldn't want diabetes medicine to cost tens of thousands of dollars a month. But then something would happen, and she'd slide right back into her Evangelical, brainwashed ways. Her metamorphosis took place over many, many lengthy conversations.

I'm not going to give myself complete credit for turning the tide; Angie's paternal grandmother was a Democrat, so those ideas could have been lurking there, latent. Angie's father's death had a huge impact on her. It changed a lot of things about how she approached her faith. Some people become more religious when someone dies or is dying, but Angie started embracing a mindset that centered on what was going on in this world, rather than spending all her time currying favor with the next. In other words, she started waxing poetic about Obama instead of faking it for Christ Jesus. To be fair, OKC leans purple, not red, so there was a palpable support for Obama, especially among young Sooners. Although in 2004, Obama initially said that "marriage is between a man and a woman" and that "we have a set of traditions in place that I think need to be preserved," he reversed course in 2012, becoming the first American president to support gay marriage. The man *evolved*.

Maybe that's why, instead of feeling like the revolution was happening worlds away, you could sense the groundswell. I knew that McCain would win Oklahoma, but for a brief minute, it felt like my whole state could turn purple for Obama, that's how charismatic the man was.

When I got Pumps an Obama sign, she put it smack-dab in the middle of her front lawn, the only house on the whole block without a McCain sign. I look back on that whole era with such nostalgia. Angie changed her voter registration to Democrat. She took a picture and sent it to me; she was so happy and proud of herself. This was during the "Yes We Can" movement, which was such an invigorating time for this country.

Sometime after that, I was sitting around Angie's house with a bunch of toddler moms. Somehow, universal health care came up. At the time, everyone was hot under the collar about this subject and whether they believed all people deserved to see good doctors to get equal care for serious illnesses. Now, I believe in universal health care, and I would happily pay more taxes to make the system accessible for everyone. But I remember the other moms saying they were against it and against paying for it, even though most of them didn't work. I remember thinking, *But I thought Jesus helped sick people.*

"But wouldn't Jesus want universal health care?" I said. "Wasn't he that type of guy?" You could feel the room hold its breath. The toddler moms sat there, blinking at me like I had ten eyes. "Don't you value helping sick, poor people over profit?"

One of them just looked me dead in the face and said, "No."

This mom was a big Bible-study regular and a rabid Republican. Ironically, her husband was a physician.

"I definitely reap the benefits of having good insurance and seeing physicians when I need to," I said. "But I don't think I'm better than anybody else for receiving health care. I think all people should have it. It's a right, not a privilege."

She looked me dead in the eye and said, "Oh, I don't think it's a right."

The diamonds cross around her neck caught the light from the chandelier. A lot of women in Oklahoma wear diamond crucifixes, which is interesting when you think about all the blood diamonds and the gross human rights violations that have occurred to get those crosses on their necks, all of which would be antithetical to the teachings of their so-called savior.

"So, you think health care should be reserved only for the privileged?" I asked.

Pumps silently chugged her sweet tea.

"Yes," she said, her big diamond-encrusted crucifix glinting. "That's right."

"Wow," I said. "This is exactly why, for multiple reasons, I'm not religious."

Pumps laughed nervously. She was used to my outbursts at this point. Remember that she grew up going to Bible study, teaching Bible study, going to church on Sundays. I don't have a problem with people that have a personal faith that they use as a source of serenity; however, the brand of Christianity in Oklahoma, and certainly in Pumps's world, was the prosperity gospel. It was more like a pyramid scheme than an avenue of growth and improvement.

"As long as you're fine with going to hell," the mom said, fingering her diamond cross.

"If that's where you think I'm going, so be it," I said, knowing I sounded very much like Julia Sugarbaker right before she gave the famous "when the lights went down in Georgia" monologue. "I'd rather be in hell with people with compassion than in heaven with coldhearted people who don't want to help sick people."

Pumps sat there, dumbfounded. Years later, she told me she secretly liked watching someone with a contrarian view buck the system. Inside her was a whole other person, like a Matryoshka doll, one who knew the lack of universal healthcare in this country was a tremendous problem. I don't know why I was so surprised. The propensity for change is always there. Pumps evolved. Obama evolved. We can *all* evolve.

But maybe we never fully escape our upbringing. People always ask me why I don't leave Oklahoma and move to a more liberal city like Los Angeles, San Francisco, or New York. As my kids have aged and become less dependent, I often ask myself the same question. I long for a big, diverse city with more museums and culture. A city packed with creative, busy people. Moving was never on the table while my kids were in school, though I flirt with the idea now that Roman is going to college.

The one impediment to this otherwise perfect plan is my parents, siblings, nieces, and nephews who live in Oklahoma. No matter what, this flawed state will always feel like home. It's not just the fleeting nature of time, something that I have come to understand now that I've put some road behind me. Time is a precious commodity and I know we don't live forever. It's why I don't feel like I have to finish books or TV shows I don't like or go out to dinner with people who annoy me to no end.

Another reason I remain tethered to OKC is my many progressive friends, who bravely fight the good fight in such a red state. During COVID, Pumps wore a Black Lives Matter mask to her kids' very Christian, mostly white school. Angie's metamorphosis has only brought us closer. Of the two of us, believe it or not, she is the big political junkie, monitoring twenty-four-hour news cycles on MSNBC like her life depends on it. I don't think it's possible to change the conservative culture of Oklahoma. It's as deeply embedded like the rest of the flaws and wonders of this great and greatly flawed country. But like the Rodgers and Hammerstein song that's basically the anthem for this ginormous, dysfunctional state, I continue to have "plen'y of heart and plen'y of hope."

MY PART IN IT

~~~~~~~~~

ANGIE

THE FIRST TIME MY parents met my ex-husband, Kirk, they begged me not to marry him. I grew up in a family where we mostly kept our thoughts and feelings to ourselves, so the sheer force of their reaction was surprising. Even though I was a good girl, the golden child, the sweetheart of Kappa Kappa Gamma, I ignored them. I probably could have married Richard Nixon, and they would have preferred it. (Truth be told, my parents liked Nixon, but that's another story.)

I know that sounds crazy. Or maybe it doesn't. Maybe it sounds like typical parent-child dynamics. Your parents don't like your choice of spouse and you blunder on, ignoring their wise counsel. But all my life, for as long as I can remember, I obsessed about my fancy wedding. I imagined living in a giant house with a bunch of kids and doing a bunch of domestic Maria von Trapp shit, like making my own graham crackers. I even had an ideal husband in mind: somebody ambitious, rich, and tall who made me laugh. Kirk seemed ambitious enough at the time; he was a successful lawyer, and we had chemistry. He was hilarious and a smart-ass. He would always open the car door for me and pull out my chair. All I wanted was to line up my pegs in that little plastic car in The Game of Life.

After six months, I decided Kirk was husband material, he had to be, even though I'd noticed a few questionable things gathering at the edge of the map. One night, right around the time we got engaged, Kirk stayed out late. Midnight came and went. Then one, two, three o'clock in the morning. I paced and smoked until I finally dozed off on the sofa. When he finally walked through the door at six a.m., he had rug burns on his knees and swollen, blistered lips. I pressed and pressed him about how the heck he got those blisters on his mouth like he'd been sucking on an exhaust pipe. He finally admitted that he'd been out with "the guys" at a bachelor party and then ended up "smoking drugs and having sex with a stripper."

Looking back, it's absolutely wild that I didn't leave his ass right then and there. It wasn't like he'd drunk one too many beers with his bros. He didn't just get a lap dance and barf in a bush. He fucked a stripper. Then he told me about it. He openly admitted to it, without hesitation. I deserved to know the truth, of course. But he didn't even consider lying to me, at least not then. Later he would lie and lie and lie but back then he must've known there would be no major consequences. I was trained to believe a wedding was my pinnacle moment, more important than graduating law school or landing a job in a prestigious law firm. Did Kirk sense I was the kind of person who cared more about the facade of a relationship than the actual relationship? Did he know I cared more about appearances than my own self-worth?

Around that time, my preacher delivered a sermon about how we bring our family's behavior into our marriages. Maybe I thought that my marriage would be like my mom and stepdad's. Somehow, I forgot to consider my husband's family and the imprint they made on him. When I think about it now, it seems naive to the point of moronic, but I lived a very sheltered existence. I didn't have a strong sense of intuition or if I did, I tamped it down, threw a frilly table-cloth over it, set a Tiffany lamp from Target on top of the tablecloth, then hung a sign over it that said *Every Day Is a Fresh Start.*

I had no one to confide in about Kirk's behavior. No one to ask, *Should I forgive him? Is this a one-off or a sign of worse things to come?*

Had I been friends with Jennifer back then, she most likely would have said, "Um, HELLO. This isn't just a sign. It's a singing sign on fire by the freeway. Wake up, bitch." But would I have listened? Who can say? At the time I thought any problems Kirk and I had would somehow magically disappear after we were married. I really believed marriage would change him. Change us. I thought marriage would expunge that night with the stripper and give our relationship a clean slate, like Febreze in a smelly bathroom. I didn't know that every problem you had before you got married gets infinitely worse afterward. If I thought he partied too much or had a penchant for strippers when we were dating, those traits only intensified after we walked down the aisle. He started going out more, spending more money. When I brought up these concerns, he assured me I was being neurotic, and everything was fine.

But this story isn't about Kirk's spending habit or his predilections, as much as my own inability to see my part in everything that happened. My stepfather came home for family dinner every night. He showed up to every game I cheered. He made sure I did my homework. He was strict but loving, a model husband to my mother. Yet when I started dating Kirk, I never asked myself, "Do I love this person? Does he love me? Is he patient and kind? Will he be a solid partner or is he self-seeking?" Looking back, I'm not sure I loved Kirk all that much, or even liked him. But I loved the idea of being loved.

One day, early on in our relationship, I hosted a lunch at Kirk's so his parents could meet my parents. I wore a dress with a full skirt and a fitted bodice and Mary Jane pumps. From a bird's-eye view, this lunch was fine, even typical. But from my parents' perspective, it was an utter disaster, indicating trouble on the horizon.

Kirk's parents weren't family-oriented like mine. They weren't what you'd call churchgoers. These days, I would never cast aspersions on a person based on how much time they spend publicly communicating with Jesus in a large, pew-lined room—I mean, look at Jennifer Welch; she wouldn't recognize Jesus if he were in line behind her at Target, and she's one of the best people I know. But back then, I have to admit it bothered me. Everyone I knew wasn't just active in their church community, it was their whole life, social or otherwise. I thought this commitment demonstrated a certain set of values, an opinion I would later come to question.

Kirk's parents were the opposite of nice. His dad was an FBI agent whose alleged affair with a reporter in Nashville had a direct effect on the Karen Silkwood case, and he ended up testifying about it before Congress. Karen Silkwood was a chemical technician who reported safety violations at a nuclear facility in Oklahoma after she discovered that she had plutonium contamination in her body and her home. Her whole story also ended up being made into a movie with Meryl Streep, Kurt Russel, and Cher. That public scandal must have affected Kirk, although he rarely discussed it. My former father-in-law was also a total hypochondriac. He would visit the doctor at least once a day and the emergency room at least twice a month. His mom ran around the house naked. The vibe of my house was chores and purity culture, and the vibe of Kirk's childhood was nudity, hypochondria, and public affairs.

At lunch that day, I remember being in a total tizzy, wanting everyone to get along, wanting my parents to approve of my fiancé. I could barely take one bite of food; I was so nervous. Everyone seemed to be getting along just fine until Kirk's mom started telling a story: She was outside grilling, and Kirk's older brother came too close to the grill. So, she grabbed a hot poker and burned him on his chest to make a point. To this day, the man still has a visible scar from essentially being branded by his own mother.

After Kirk's mom finished telling this doozy of a tale, my future ex-father-in-law and future ex-husband started laughing hysterically. But my parents sat there, mortified. I think my mom said, "That's not funny." Or maybe she said nothing, but I could tell what she was thinking by the way she looked at me wide-eyed, like a hare. The rest of the meal was unremarkable. We talked about sports and the weather. Kirk was unusually attentive. I thought, *This will all work out. This will be my life. Sunday lunches with my in-laws and my parents. Kirk will become a devoted family man who keeps his pickle where it belongs: in his pants. I will become my mother and make five-course dinners every night after working on my feet all day. I will brown the chicken and mash the potatoes and we will go to church on Sundays.*

The next time I went to my parents' house for dinner, I'd barely rested my purse on the front-hall table before my mom said, "Angie, you have got to get away from that man. His parents are emotionally unwell. He's incapable of being the kind of husband you need."

I remember I laughed, but they didn't.

"They're making light of something inappropriate that should be disturbing to you," my stepdad added. "Your mother and I left lunch alarmed. This isn't a good sign." I started to say something, but he interrupted me. "Your mother and I don't think anything good can come from being married to that man."

I didn't know what to say. On at least two other occasions before the wedding, when my parents tried to tell me that I was making a huge mistake, maybe the hugest of my life, it was like they were speaking to me in Romanian. We'd already sent out the save-the-date cards and made a deposit on the venue. I was in the den with my mother, watching the 1937 Fred Astaire/Ginger Rogers vehicle *Shall We Dance*. For those of you who don't watch a lot of Fred and Ginger movies, that's the one where they sing "Let's Call the Whole Thing Off" and then do a tap dance number on roller skates. After the song ended, my mother said something rhetorical like, "Wasn't that amazing? There wasn't anybody like Fred Astaire." Then my stepdad announced he and my mother wouldn't feel good about themselves as parents if they didn't tell *me* to call the whole thing off. They just had a premonition that Kirk was slicker than owl poop.

I remember thinking, *But what about all those cocktail napkins we just ordered with our names and the date on them for passed hors d'oeuvres?* We were on a greased chute to our wedding; plans were in motion, and I couldn't stop them. It was like I was on the Big Bend at Six Flags Fiesta, shooting down the straight-away into a crowded swimming pool.

So, I suppressed my inner voice, the one that said, *WAKE UP, YOUR PARENTS ARE RIGHT*. I went ahead and walked down the aisle in that white dress looking like a cake topper. I had no idea how often my then-husband was paying countless women to go heels to Jesus with him. His obsession with sex workers would later cost him his children, my sanity, our savings, and our house. At the time, I was dumb as an ostrich, but my parents could smell future trouble in the air like the sulfurous odor of a twister sweeping off the plains.

At our wedding, a five-hundred-person affair, I knew in my heart I was making a big mistake; I felt it in my bones. It lined the stays of my dress and contained the tulle of my veil. I saw it on my parents' faces—even on the face of my biological father who was a more open-minded, forgiving guy. That morning, I started drinking at 11 a.m. All my sorority sisters thought I was just being my usual fun, party self, but I couldn't shake the feeling that I was a sacrificial lamb being led to the slaughter. What could I do? Turn to my cousin and say, "Kirk spends an unusual amount of time at titty bars, Linda. Help me sneak out before I walk down the aisle and ruin the rest of my life." The train hadn't just left the station, it had left the country.

I had nine bridesmaids in red dresses, two designated candle-lighters, and two guestbook-holders, dressed in purple. It was like Austin Powers and Queen Elizabeth dopped acid and birthed a coronation in OKC. As I walked down that aisle, I could practically feel each step bringing me closer to oblivion. This denial formed the warp and weft of my marriage. I had wanted God to give me a sign, like water turning into wine, or a talking fish. But the type of sign I got didn't fit my chosen narrative. And the narrative, I believed, was immutable.

Kirk gave me my three wonderful kids, and I will always be grateful for that, even as I prayed for a colony of fire ants to crawl up his dickhole. Sometimes, I think about what I would tell my daughter if she brought another Kirk home. Would I call on Jennifer for backup or would I tell Emily to go for it and let her make her own mistakes? I think the latter.

Ultimately, despite it all, like a bad tattoo, I have no regrets. Fine, my parents were right all along. But every mistake has taught me a lesson, made me stronger and wiser, if poorer and older. I needed to fail. The narrative needed to fail, before I could write a new, more authentic story.

MAKE YOUR OWN MONEY, HONEY

JEN

MY YOUNGER SON, ROMAN, has been obsessed with basketball since he was four years old. Now that he plays varsity, I try to attend all if not most of his games. Often, I go with my husband or my parents, even if it's an away game, which can be a major commitment, considering the size of our great state. For instance, the other day, I drove all the way to Jones, Oklahoma—a two-hour drive through what I like to call "Real Oklahoma"—to watch Roman's team play the Chandler Lions.

Roman attends a secular private school. His basketball team plays schools all across the state, especially as the season progresses from sectionals to regionals. Now, I have nothing against public schools; in fact, I support them wholeheartedly. I wish our leaders valued education in this country as much as they value war and guns. I want my kid's education to instill critical thinking and his history and science lessons to have depth and breadth. I want my child to be inspired to read more and to be curious about the art and culture of our wider world.

However, I want to add that I am not against a bit of shit-talk in sports. It keeps everyone on their toes. But when my son and the rest of the starting lineup stepped onto that court, the opposing team started chanting, "Daddy's money! Daddy's money!" That made me madder than a hornet. Those children had their shit-talk all wrong. My husband's money didn't pay for one cent of Roman's education. My interior design business paid for my children's tuition (secondary school and college), our mortgage, and all four car payments. It paid for our vacations, airfare, and hotel rooms. If only they'd been chanting, "Mommy's money. Mommy's money," I wouldn't be writing this little screed about the sexist injustices of Trump-loving, white America otherwise known as MAGA. But here we are, reader.

Here we fucking are.

Still, that chant got me to thinking about my own daddy. From the time he was seven years old, my dad's passion had always been racing pigeons. He joined an international community of people who breed and train pigeons.

In fact, he and his cronies still spend a large chunk of their weekends driving five hundred miles from my parents' house and setting the birds free to race them home.

In the eighties, when the oil and real estate markets crashed, everyone we knew went from upper middle class to broke.

Somehow, my father got the brilliant idea to turn his pigeon-breeding hobby into an income stream. He looked at my mother and said, "You know, I'm going to start selling my birds."

My mother rolled her eyes because the pigeons already occupied most of my dad's time and attention. He spent many meals talking about each individual bird as if they were family members. Dinner was like an episode of *Dallas*, but with pigeons as Bobby and Pamela Ewing. Over time, he became the world's largest breeder and seller of racing pigeons.

Believe it or not, there's a sizable international market for racing pigeons. The bane of my mother's existence ultimately made our family a ton of money, and she ended up helping him run what became the family business. My mother was a very intellectual woman and an independent thinker. She read widely across all genres. I often think she would have been a wonderful English literature professor or a writer. But my father needed her meticulous bookkeeping and keen eye for detail, so she suppressed her own needs and desires to work for him, kowtowing to his every whim. In as much as the pendulum of adult life swings between acceptance and resentment, my mother just did what she had to do. She never articulated her desire to get more from life than balancing columns of numbers in a ledger and tallying these columns with other columns. I wondered if, sometimes, as she washed dishes in the kitchen, she looked out into the yard and thought about a different life, a life that revolved around something more creative and challenging, something with actual human colleagues and ideas, not birds. But she remained indebted to my father financially. I knew I didn't want to be indebted to anyone. I knew the only solution was to have my own money. I learned how to do that because I saw my father do it with a bunch of birds in our backyard.

Of course, when I was a child, I didn't fully understand that it was much harder for women to achieve financial stability than it was for men to do the same, or that it was even harder for women of color than white women, who were more likely to have accrued generational wealth. I just knew I had to be financially independent. My mom taught me from an early age to examine the world from all angles—history, politics, religion—including, and most significantly, the way God demands worship like some narcissistic boyfriend. She taught me not to give a hoot what anyone else thought. She also taught me that the Bible is many things: an enduring work of literature, a metaphorical war epic, and an epic bestseller. Mostly, she taught me to respect all people and to be curious about the world beyond Oklahoma.

So, you can imagine her unorthodox way of thinking contrasted with the general character of the Bible Belt. While my mother yammered that people should be freethinkers, her actions implied a wholly different alignment—not to herself but to my dad and his every need.

During high school, I was busy trying to figure out the delicate balance of my own social life, coming home from cheerleading practice or going to church with any number of my friends who were constantly trying to "save" me. The complexity of adult life and marriage seemed abstract, though

I did start to see both my parents as fallible. Years later, I would wonder, were they just exhibiting attributes common to Baby Boomers, or was this the unique nature of their marriage? Did they sometimes imagine they were married to other people? Did my mother look at the wide sky and wish she was one of my father's birds, driven five hundred miles away and set free, only to return to the same place, time and time again?

And what about my ancestors? I'd wash dishes, thinking about my great-great-great-great-great-great-great-grandmother. Her shorter lifespan and how she likely put less of a premium on personal happiness. Did she feel stuck? Did she also want more out of life? Or was she only worrying about procuring venison and drying lingonberries before the long, harsh winter?

After Roman was born, I had two small kids at home, and Josh very briefly became the breadwinner. The only glitch in this otherwise perfect plan was that Josh was a walking financial catastrophe. Like many addicts, especially in the early days of recovery, he struggled to maintain sobriety. Also, like many addicts, his finances could be a bit . . . *messy*. I found that it was better if I worked. I built my interior design business not only on my creative talent but also on my drive to provide for my family. It was preferable for me to get up at five in the morning and pick out toss pillows and sofas for people instead of panicking about the size of Josh's paycheck and what he was doing with it. I'd helped my dad clean the pigeon loft in high school then waited tables off and on at

Chili's throughout college and early adulthood. I knew what it was like to work hard, to get up early in the morning to do chores in the loft or to stay late to marry the ketchups at Chili's. I'd stood on my feet, taking people's orders, and bringing them extra sauce for their Triple Dipper or Baby Back Ribs.

When I got into interior design, I worked full-time for another designer for two years. But then people started contacting me, friends of friends, asking "Will you help me do this? Will you help me do that?" I took on every project, even if somebody had a small budget. I had the capitalist mindset that business was business and money was money. I would never say no to anybody with a checkbook. I returned phone calls. I returned emails. I did my best, even when I had imposter syndrome. I often had a voice in my head, which I describe as "cinder blocks sitting atop my shoulders, raining hellfire on my psyche." Sounds fun, right? In the very first days of starting my business, I had about ten on each shoulder. But I felt that if I just returned every email and every phone call, if I kept trying to get as much done as I could every day, those blocks would weigh a little less the next day. I discovered the only antidote for my impostor syndrome was a combination of blind faith, trust, and experience. I had to act as if I knew what I was doing until I racked up those experience points. I had to act as if I was as sure of myself as one of my dad's birds, flying their way home.

My decision to make my own money was empowering. It created distance between Josh's behavior and my financial dependence on him. And it also helped me protect our kids. That way, if Josh had to go to rehab for three months, six months, even a year, we wouldn't have to move into the pigeon loft.

However you interpret my marriage or my finances, it's my deep-seated belief that you've got to make your own money, honey. Money is bigger than the stuff you buy. Don't get me wrong. I'm as vapid and shallow as the next person. I sell overpriced furniture and pick out statement chandeliers for the one percent. It doesn't get shallower than that, but having money gave me emotional freedom. It gave me space and safety. It was one less thing to worry about. Living with a person with a substance-use disorder could be the very definition of *feast or famine*. The ground constantly shifted like an active fault line. Josh was in and out of rehab a total of five times before he got sober for good. The first time, in 2003, I could barely scrape together enough money to pay utility bills and buy diapers. Financial precarity on top of loving an addict caused debilitating anxiety that felt like being on Space Mountain without a safety belt. This feeling—that I could tumble from the ride into darkness—stayed with me for years, a tentacular clutch on my mind, heart, and stomach.

Pumps stayed in her marriage much longer than she would have if she'd kept her job. But she stopped working as a lawyer when she had kids. When she discovered how often that husband of hers had been batter-dipping the corn dog, she had zero recourse. After all those years out of work, she was behind the eight ball. There was no way she could carry the mortgage and all three tuitions, plus all the other sundry expenses. I've seen this happen so many times—people, most often women, who are trapped in bad marriages to keep their kids fed and a roof over their heads. I realize people's marital and financial situations are much more complex than I'm sketching here. I would never be so glib as to say, "Why don't they just leave?" But I do know that once I started betting on myself, the money followed. It's not selfish to indulge your career aspirations. In my experience, it's been one of the essential linchpins of my family's happiness.

My income protected my kids from their father's worst demons—the most compelling case I had for making my own money. I was able to kick Josh out to protect them. If I hadn't been financially successful, if I hadn't believed in my ability to provide for myself and for them, my kids would've seen the worst parts of their father's addiction and the scariest parts of my sorrow and fear. Instead, they're a lot more like the best parts of him, the kind, funny, intelligent, sober parts. The parts Josh had to dig deep to find and work hard to discover.

I briefly went to Al-Anon but found individual therapy more helpful. Sitting in those rooms, I recognized that work saved my life. Both of my sons witnessed my dedication and resolve. They saw me working hard to put money on the table to provide for our family. At the time, I didn't realize how hard I was working to keep everybody above sea level, myself included. My work kept me from going off the deep end, even though starting my business was daunting. This is a value I try to instill in my sons. The value of showing up to do the work, even when you'd rather watch TV, play video games, or party with your friends. Michelle Obama once said that she'd told Sasha and Malia, "Every day is an opportunity to practice who we want to become," meaning that every little thing we do sets up a pattern to continue being better.

I remember thinking, *If this phone doesn't ring, and I don't get new jobs, I won't have money for the kids' school.* But now when I turn back and look at it, I think, *You did that. You worked your ass off and then got noticed, and you ended up on Bravo, a skinny little ol' gal from Oklahoma City. You have a podcast that you show up to do something for every day. People besides your blood relatives listen to it. You got to be on* The Today Show *and* CNN.

I'll admit that in some of those early design projects, I hadn't quite grasped the idea that less is more. I hadn't developed a signature style. I painted every room a different color. I was *unleashed.* Two or three years later, a client might want to change up their toss pillows or recover an accent chair that the dog peed on. I'd walk into their houses, and I'd think, *Holy Mother of God, it looks like Elton John threw up in here. I need to lay off the paint deck and be a bit more classic.* Now instead of feeling inadequate, I laugh and have a private gut check. I tell myself it was the nineties and the tassels had tassels.

Watching Roman running the length of the court filled me with such joy. My boy, almost a man. He seemed so focused and strong and sure of himself. The clock was running down on the first half, and our team was crushing. I recognized a lot of the moms in the stands, and we all gave each other a look that said, "Please let us win this game so that my child is in a good mood when he comes home."

I thought I would be happy no longer having to drive Roman everywhere, but believe me, having your teenager in a car on the freeway in a vehicle that he is controlling is its own fresh hell. Next year, he will be in college, investing in his own dreams. Perhaps he will become an attorney like his father. I can see him studying hard, taking responsibility for his future, like his older brother, Dylan, a journalism major at Syracuse.

In the end, we beat the Lions, which made me want to jump up and yell, "How's that for Mommy's money, *honey*?" But I didn't. I just winked at Roman, mouthed, *Nice job*, thanked his coach, and went to my car. I know I can keep learning and improving. I need to.

I'm betting on myself to win.

SISTER, SISTER

~~~~~~~~~~~

ANGIE

THIS MIGHT BE A completely retro thing to say, but I loved my sorority, Kappa Kappa Gamma, more than life itself. I still love it. Those girls were my chosen family. Maybe it's because college was such a formative time, the way some of my East Coast friends describe their experiences at summer camp, but as soon as I got to University of Oklahoma, I felt like I had found my people. And my wild child was unleashed.

OU is very Greek; there are about four thousand students in the Greek system out of twenty thousand total. It felt like everybody we knew was in the Greek system. We thought we ran the whole school. Back in the day of the dinosaurs, we girls couldn't drink in our sorority houses, but the boys could drink in theirs, which seems so backward now, but then it seemed normal, I guess. Somebody was having a party every single night. It was a free-for-all, the opposite of my adolescence in purity culture, which was a combination of cheerleading, going to church, and working at my parents' convenience store, where my stepdad made fried chicken and fried burritos, all that junky, delicious shit. You haven't lived until you've had a fried burrito smothered in extremely hot queso. My parents expected me to work at their store, so I didn't have much free time to get in trouble. I went there to mop the floor, clean up the kitchen, wipe down the frying area. Sometimes, if I was lucky, I'd run the cash register.

Strict parents in purity culture are a whole different breed of strict. It's *STRICT* with a capital strict. My mother was raised in an ultrareligious home, where scripture was the main form of entertainment. She grew up going to church on Wednesdays and twice on Sundays. She never drank and I wouldn't know if she had sex before she procreated. I would rather turn into a pillar of salt than ask her. I would rather be banned from the ark. All the arks. I would rather watch *Heaven's Gate*. I would rather go to Disney on Ice every night for the rest of my life.

In high school, I hardly drank and if I did, I nursed a peach Bartles & Jaymes and felt guilty about it. I kept my grades up. I wasn't allowed to talk on the phone for more than a very brief, prescribed amount of time. This was during landline days, so it was easy for my parents to monitor my phone usage when they were home. Jennifer was allowed to have her own teenage phone line, but my parents would never have given me that type of freedom.

When I got to campus, I knew I had to rush Kappa Kappa Gamma. They were a top-tier sorority with the best girls and the best parties, something I knew very little about. It wasn't that I wanted to do a total one-eighty—Kappa Kappa Gamma was mostly Christian girls from Texas and Oklahoma—but I knew that without my mom and stepdad I could finally drink, mess around with boys, and not get in trouble. I still feared tarnishing my reputation in their eyes. Maybe the elevator didn't reach the top, but I still needed my parents to think I was still God's golden angel.

During work week, which is the period leading up to rush week, I really clicked with all the other gals rushing KKG. As soon as I got in, I spent the next four years in a haze of underage drinking and kissing boys. Each fraternity invited a certain sorority to be their little sisters, which in retrospect sounds infantilizing, but at the time, felt fun. We were the little sisters of Alpha Tau Omega. ATO threw all these themed parties like Kite and Key, and Champagne Jam. I know I must have studied and gone to class occasionally, because making good grades was part of the Kappa Kappa Gamma holy covenant—plus I got into law school—but I honestly could not tell you a single thing I read or learned. I can barely remember the name of any of my classes. I just remember cramming for exams and tailgating at Sooners games and the very ill-fitting dress I wore to the Rose Ball formal. (Again, it was the eighties, so you can just imagine the jewel tones and the shoulder pads. Oh, and the Aqua Net. Don't forget the Aqua Net. I think KKG is singlehandedly responsible for blowing a hole in the ozone layer.)

Sometimes, listening to my sorority sisters gabbing on the hall phone with their mothers, I felt jealous of the easy camaraderie that seemed so evident between them. Most of these girls had the same kind of upbringing I did. Yet, somehow it seemed like they weren't as sheltered as I was. We were all so excited to drink and get laid at college. Why did it seem like all my friends spoke so openly to their mothers about their dating shenanigans? They told their mothers who they were kissing or who had rejected them. My mother used to pitch a fit if I showed even a hint of a bra strap, let alone if my date said boo. But remember, I was raised in a Dickensian world of pure or impure, good or bad, right or wrong. There was no "We trust you to figure out the vicissitudes of life, Angie." I had all my vicissitudes figured out by my parents, who'd had theirs figured by their pastor who had his figured by the Good Lord. Amen.

I can vividly remember getting dressed to go to the OU/ Texas party in Dallas. I remember putting on my Benetton sweater, applying lip gloss, and blow-drying then teasing my hair, but I don't recall any of the boys I kissed. They're mostly all a blur. I do remember all my sisters getting dressed together, laughing. I remember dreaming of one day calling my daughter and having one of these best-gal-pal conversations, like I heard my KKG sisters have with their mothers. I vowed that when I had a daughter, I would be the type of mother she could call and talk about her dating life.

I graduated from college in May with a degree in elementary education, and then the following September, I applied to law school, even though my mother repeatedly told me being a lawyer was a man's job. Even as an undergrad, I was interested in criminal law and planned to pursue pre-law as my bachelor's degree. When I called my mom to inform her, she snorted and said, "That's the most ridiculous degree in the world. You can't get a job doing anything with that."

"Mom," I said, "I literally can be a lawyer."

But my mother wanted me to be a preschool teacher. She was operating under the Silent Generation/Boomer mentality that women can only be secretaries, nurses, or teachers. I value all those jobs. I have the highest respect for teachers. We need teachers and nurses more than we need lawyers, that's for damn sure. But after my short stint student-teaching fifth grade, I knew I wasn't cut out for teaching. I just knew I didn't have that level of patience. I secretly took the GRE and the LSAT, and then I applied to law school. I didn't even tell my mom I was going until three days before I left on a backpacking trip to Europe. We were out at dinner, and I said, "Hey, I'm leaving in three days to travel through Europe and then I'm starting law school in August."

"Okay," my mom said through a big bite of her chicken-fried steak.

The funny thing is I didn't understand the depths of my mother's ironclad desire for my future until decades later, when I desperately wanted my own daughter, Emily, to rush Kappa Kappa Gamma when she got into OU. This need drove me like a third rail. I don't think I would have been any happier if she had won a Nobel Prize or I had won the lottery. At that point in the trajectory of my life, I'd just gone back to work as a divorce lawyer after being a stay-at-home power mom for more than a decade. Annoyingly, while I was following Emily around the house or driving her to The Container Store, buying her all the Simplehuman stuff she needed for her dorm room, flapping my lips about how rushing KKG would change her whole life, Emily seemed ambivalent. I'd go into her room to put her laundry away and start singing, *"I'm so happy that I am a Kappa Kappa Gamma."*

But Emily only rolled her eyes at me and went back to scrolling TikTok, anything to shut me out, just as I shut out my mother before her. If I wasn't careful, Emily might end up transferring to some East Coast school that didn't even have Greek life and where everyone was a Wiccan or a folk singer with hairy armpits. At night, I would get on the group chat with my sorority sisters, lost in a well of memories. **Remember the night of the Tennessee game? Remember the trip to New Orleans when we danced at AT2s, and I puked bright red hurricanes all over Bourbon Street like I was Linda Blair in The Exorcist? Remember that first warm spring night we danced barefoot in the rain? Remember, remember, remember, remember?**

Kids are going to do their own thing, no matter how much you say, "Look at all these nice girls rushing OU, doing those fun choreographed dances, talking about their bracelets from Claire's. Aren't they so gosh-darn cute? Don't you want to be friends with them?" I had to learn through experience that my job as a parent isn't to create goals for my kids and then push them over the line. It's to equip them with the tools to create their own.

I believe the same instinct holds true for all relationships. Even when we know what's right for our family and friends, the most we can do is share our advice and encouragement and offer our support. The less I graft my ambitions, desires, and dreams onto the lives of my loved ones the better. Those are sacred spaces for them to cultivate and nurture on their own.

Of course, all of this was darn near impossible for me to recognize when I was trying to get my children to do something I KNEW was the right thing to do, or I KNEW would make them so happy, like rushing Kappa Kappa Gamma.

My first sponsor in AA once said, "Unfulfilled expectations make you fucking cuckoo." What she meant was you can want things, but expectations can cause major disappointment and therefore hardcore suffering. Most of us have an attachment to praise and aversion to criticism (and, for sure, a mighty aversion to our moms telling us what sorority to rush). When you achieve your goals, such as graduating from college or getting into law school, you may experience that hot blip of dopamine. Or you may feel the cold slap of disappointment if you don't land a spot in your top-choice law firm. The good news is you can set new goals. Plant ten seeds and the eleventh one will grow. You just can't get too attached to how the garden will look. Or if everyone will even like it. I spent so much time trying to grow other people's gardens, trying to change them instead of changing how I reacted to them, which is the only thing you *can* change, yourself.

What this all came down to is my relationship to control. There are certain elements of my life I can account for. I can show up for those I love. I can work hard, treat my body with respect, spread kindness, tip well, and vote Democrat. But ultimately, I can't control how others perceive me. I can't control how they organize their own lives. With my support and brilliant maternal guidance, I can only gently suggest or influence. But that's about it.

Ultimately, Emily rushed KKG. Mazel tov! Confetti! Rejoice! Her sorority went viral on TikTok for doing a dance dressed up as Smurfs. All was right with my world. Then—Whac-A-Mole! Despair!—other life problems cropped up because they always do. The lazy Susan of shit sandwiches continued to dish up the doo-doo.

One day, my girl will know the painful longing only nostalgia brings. My memories from thirty-five years ago are more vivid than something that happened just this morning. She will know crow's-feet and belly rolls and creaky knees. If she decides to have babies, she will know what it's like to want them to have all the good things she had and then some. The education, the clothes, the house, the love. She will have dreams for those babies. But she'll have to learn the hard way, like I did, like my mother did, that her children will have their own dreams. A life that's theirs to craft. I can fly beside her for as long as she'll allow it, but at some point, isn't it better to let her find her own way out of the nest and into the world? And isn't it better to say, "I did my best." Isn't it better to allow my daughter to live the life I didn't have, making her own stupid mistakes?

If that moment comes, I'll be there to support my daughter's babies—or pets!—no matter what. But still, I hope they all rush Kappa Kappa Gamma.

FOR THE BIRDS

~~~~~~~~

JEN

RECENTLY, I'VE BEEN THINKING a lot about legacy. Not in terms of last will and testament, though maybe that too. You can't help but get teary doing any sort of estate planning when you're a parent, imagining your progeny hanging your artwork in their homes and saying to their kids, "This was your grandmother's. She commissioned this painting of Obama. She also had exquisite taste and stayed fit and healthy till the end."

But what really lingers on the forefront of my mind these days is the type of emotional future I've established for my sons. Did I build them a house of bricks or a house of straw? Will the shelter I've created for them weather all the storms of adulthood? Because if you've lived more than a month of Sundays, you know that life can throw you for a goddamn loop, but it can also take you on a wild ride up the coast. When Josh was actively using, I wouldn't allow him to live with us. On his third relapse, I decided that the only way I was going to let him back into our home was if he passed a hair follicle test, which determines whether a person has consumed alcohol or drugs in the past ninety days. It was a tough decision but one which I ultimately felt was best for me and my sons. I wanted to spare them as much unpredictability and difficulty as I possibly could.

Addiction is by nature a selfish disease, whether the addict is in the throes of untreated alcoholism or is the owner of a ten-year chip. At its peak, it forces the nonaddict partner to bear the brunt of all the difficult decisions and depressive episodes. I know I did the right thing and I also know everything we do or don't do has repercussions. This is all a part of being human. They should have a pamphlet on how to handle the emotional fallout of addiction at the doctor's office next to the brochures about insomnia and diabetes prevention, or the signs about how to detect if you have colorectal cancer. How to make sure your kids made it through the world of adulthood unscathed by their parents' fuckups. At night, I would lie in bed wondering if I'd done enough to insulate my boys from my and Josh's issues. Had I blocked the curse through the sheer force of my maternal will? Or was it codependent to think I had any power to affect anything beyond the orbit of my own experience? My legacy.

Recently, my mother called me to discuss Crackers, my dad's beloved African grey parrot. The question at hand was which of my siblings would assume the awesome responsibility for the care of Crackers after my parents left this mortal coil. Now, my parents are real animal people. So am I. We all love our dogs. But parrots live to be eighty darn years old. I did not want to get stuck listening to Crackers cuss or cleaning its cage for the next thirty years. These birds are messy and incredibly smart. The whole line of conversation reminded me of an episode of *Curb Your Enthusiasm*. Was Crackers the sum total of my parents' estate? A bird that will never die?

Now that he's retired, my dad is as passionate about Crackers as he is about his racing pigeons, meaning he loves Crackers like another child. He still keeps a ton of pigeons in the loft he built in his backyard. When I was a teenager, I wanted to live closer to town so I could be nearer to my friends, but to keep those giant lofts, we needed a whole lot more acreage and so we lived further out in the suburbs. Did I resent my dad for this strange habit that also put food on the table? Maybe. But everyone in Oklahoma was struggling financially after the oil market crashed. My dad had such enthusiasm for those birds. He also wasn't the kind of dad who took kindly to rebellion, so I mostly did what I was supposed to do. It wasn't that I feared my father as much as I'm not sure I knew him. A shadow surrounded him from his time in Vietnam, an era I knew little about except what I saw in movies like *Platoon*. The shadow created an opacity that often made my dad unreachable. Now that we know more about PTSD and how it affects the body, these issues are more likely to be treated therapeutically, but like so many men of his generation, my father just got on with it. My mother, my siblings, and I bore the brunt of his quiet rage by predicting his moods telepathically and responding accordingly. I knew when to speak and also when to avoid my dad and go to my room to do my homework.

But when I was with my dad in that loft with his pigeons, we bonded over their feed and care. The way my father spoke to them and cradled them lovingly gave me a pang. Watching the tenderness and wisdom on display was like a scene from a Disney movie, where I half expected the pigeons to start singing a wise and jolly song. My dad could differentiate each one from the next, their habits and weaknesses, especially the ones that won races. Sometimes I wondered, did he know me that well? My skills and talents? My defects?

"People have been using pigeons for communication for five thousand years," he once told a friend of mine. We were standing in the yard, gazing at the lofts. She'd inquired about the difference between city birds and his award-winning flock.

"That's like comparing an ass to a thoroughbred," he said, and she laughed. I wasn't sure he was being funny but that was also his humor, dry and truthful as the Plains.

I get my business acumen and drive from my father. And my stubbornness, which is either a boon or a flaw depending on the day or the situation. My mother is an intellectual but a total pushover. If you need someone to be your ally, my stubbornness is a biological weapon, but if you're my spouse and you're in an argument with me, it's a barbed sword dipped in dung, passed down to me from my father and his father's father. What do my sons, Dylan and Roman, see when I'm at my worst? What will they say about me in their therapy sessions? Where will they aim the laser pointer when analyzing what happened between me and their father? What indelible defect will the awl of memory scrawl on their interactions?

Recent studies on humans and animals suggest that trauma can leave a mark on your genes, and those genetic markers can be passed down to subsequent generations. Meaning: your ancestors can affect who you are, even if you never met them. If your grandmother lived through the terrible wars or famine or the Holocaust or survived the Armenian genocide or dysentery on the Oregon Trail, some aspect of those traumas could live on in her cellular makeup and, subsequently, in the makeup of her progeny and her progeny's progeny. Did my emotional legacy imply that I was forever fucked? Or is Freud correct in claiming that because we have parents, we're all fucked? (I'm obviously paraphrasing.) Can we ever put our ancestral trauma to bed?

How many times had I watched my dad taking care of Crackers? How many times had I seen my dad feed that bird and change its water? One day, my mom called me at work.

"Jennifer, I have some alarming news," she said.

"What is it?" I said, my heart racing as I prepared for the worst.

"Crackers laid an egg."

"I thought Crackers was a boy?" I said.

"You can imagine my surprise," my mother said in her signature dry, Texas deadpan and we both laughed.

"I guess I have a sister," I said.

At night, as my dad walked the perimeter of the house, checking that the doors were all locked, he dropped a cloth over Cracker's cage to simulate the darkness of her native habitat. African greys are very sensitive to human feelings and events. They witness everything that occurs in a household and can even provide probable cause or evidence to a police officer in criminal proceedings. I recently read about a parrot named Bud who mimicked the last words of a murdered man begging for his life. The parrot's "testimony" helped the police figure out that it wasn't an intruder who killed him, but the man's own wife. Crackers had heard so many family secrets over the years. She'd heard the fights and seen the silent recriminations. Would Crackers become the moral center of our family? Would she be the arbiter of my marital disputes? Maybe one day she'd deliver my dad's eulogy.

The intersection between Cracker's memory and overcoming family trauma lies in her ability to repeat words or phrases that echo moments of emotional intensity. A parrot's memory can linger, bringing the past into the present through repetition. The bird's mimicry serves as an unsettling reminder of unresolved tensions, yet its mechanical recollection contrasts with the more human process of healing. While a parrot echoes the past unchanged, the challenge for humans is to transform memory into understanding, allowing for release and growth, otherwise known as catharsis.

In the summer of 2024, one of Roman's best friends from childhood drowned in an accident at Grand Lake. Every molecule in Roman's body grieved and ached for his friend. Our whole family felt the acute pain of this tragic death deep in our bones, the way anyone would when a bright young person's life is suddenly cut short. Like any grandfather, my dad was extremely worried about his grandson and called me frequently to check in on him. One day, he called just as I landed at Will Rogers Airport and was loading my suitcases into my car. My dad asked how I was doing and inquired after Roman, but I could tell by the deliberate way he was pausing he had more on his mind.

"I've never told you this," he said. "In fact, I don't think I've told anyone, but my friend from high school was killed in Vietnam. He was shot, and I was with him. I still think about it a lot, but you know . . . we just—we just never talked about these things."

As I pulled onto the interstate, the Oklahoma sky bright and blue above me, I said, "I'm so sorry that happened, Dad. And I'm sorry you've held that in for so long. It must really hurt."

These are the words we say to someone to express our empathy for their grief. "I'm sorry." But what are we sorry for? How many young men did my dad witness die in battle? It overwhelmed me to think about all the pain he'd kept buried inside all these decades. That five-minute phone call was the most real moment I'd ever had with my father. Did that revelation heal everything that ever happened to him or cleanse everything he saw in Vietnam? Did it change everything between us? I know that's impossible. But it felt healing, or at least like the process had begun. I wanted the same catharsis for Roman more than I'd wanted anything in my life; I wanted it for my dad, for all of us.

But as I sat with the weight of all this senseless death, I reminded myself of another scientific reality. Nothing is static or fixed, not even that damn bird. Our cells regenerate every seven years. Even if I'm theoretically living with inherited generational traumas, and possibly passing them on to my kids, their cells (and mine) are resilient. We make our own story. A family never recognizes its happiest moments even while it's drinking its sweet tea or tearing open its PlayStation on Christmas morning. It only recognizes the import of those seemingly meaningless moments later when the parrot is squawking, "Don't shoot," or the money runs out. Then everyone sits around wishing they could go back to those happy times they didn't even know were happy. What I do have is this life, right now, and with it, the opportunity, each day, to create a fresh narrative, a different story. A rich legacy of all the laughter and all the tears. The fights and the fond farewells. All the vomit, the poo-poo diapers, the carpooling, the cigarettes, the fights, the private jokes, the sex in the pantry, and the greasy all-you-can-eat pizza. If in the end, my kids remember more of the good than the bad, that's a win in my book.

And that damn bird will probably outlive us all.

SHAME IS A MISERABLE LIFE PARTNER

ANGIE

WHEN MY KIDS WERE little, I took them to the AMC at the Quail Springs Mall to see *The Hobbit*. To be honest, I'm not a big fan of fantasy fiction. Real talk: I've never actually read any Tolkien. I only like upmarket fiction about messy lives with redemption arcs, or nonfiction books where they mercilessly trash Trump. So, I was mostly planning to look at my phone and eat popcorn and Sour Patch Kids for three hours.

Somehow, as I was half watching the movie, half scrolling my phone, I got pulled into the story of Bilbo Baggins and his magical, mystical adventure. When Bilbo falls into a crevice at the root of the Misty Mountains and encounters Gollum, the slimy creature who dwells in an underground lake, I found myself strangely hooked. I won't go into the whole plot because I only understood about half of it, but a game of trickery ensues where Bilbo ends up with the Ring and escapes under a cloak of invisibility. The dumpy middle-aged hobbit triumphed!

Afterward, we went for all-you-can-eat pizza at Mazzio's. The week passed in its usual way: Kirk worked. I made breakfast, lunch, multiple snacks, and dinner. I cleaned the kitchen, put away the toys, did the laundry, and drove the kids to and from school, soccer practice, and their friends' houses. I went grocery shopping at Albertsons and Trader Joe's. Emily was very into dance at the time, so I took her to the dance studio and sewed sequins onto her halter tops and hot-glued rhinestones onto her puffy headbands. I baked chocolate chip cookies for the soccer team bake sale and made potato salad for the church picnic. The whole time, I couldn't get the slimy creature at the bottom of the rock out of my mind.

For the duration of our marriage, Kirk and I were supposedly "in therapy." We started going pretty much from the rip over our communication issues. He thought he should be able to stay out all hours of the night doing Lord-only-knows-what. I thought I should be able to wander the house in my robe and slippers, oscillating between passive-aggressive dusting and aggressive-passive tidying. In order to resuscitate our marriage, our pastor suggested we try counseling. If someone recommended that to me now, I would say, "Oh, this marriage has a DNR. No heroic measures necessary." But back then I didn't have an advanced directive. I performed heroic measures. I intubated, I defibrillated, I performed a thoracotomy, then a heart and liver transplant.

It makes me laugh to think of it now, because when I say Kirk and I were *in therapy*, I mean we physically went to an office where we sat on opposite sides of a sofa, glowering at a psychologist. And we sat on that sofa for *fifteen years*. Our mouths opened and closed, and words came out of them, but we weren't talking or listening to each other. The words floated around the room and evaporated into the air. As soon as the clock started, Kirk would launch into the same song and dance, reiterating the same crap: "I'm behind at work, I'm worried about money, and there's not enough time for me to do all the things I have to do at work. Blah blah blah." Sometimes the complaint would be at me, but usually, we were both facing forward, like we were watching a movie, while Kirk talked at our audience of one, aka our therapist.

I sat on the other end of the couch and thought, *If you're not going to do anything about it, about us, why the fuck are we here?* Sometimes I said that out loud, and we got into a fight. The therapist said something therapeutic like, "How does that make you feel, Kirk?"

"I feel fine," Kirk said or something equally stupid and dishonest. He glared at me like how could I not understand all the problems and conditions of being a Great Man? All the wars and the hunting and the gathering. The *sacrifices* he was making to keep our little family afloat. I glared right back at him. Two could play at that game, motherfucker. I also have a PhD in passive-aggression at this point.

"Obviously you don't, Kirk," I said. Or something equally brilliant. "It's not my fault you're stressed out. Maybe if you didn't '*go out*' so much, you wouldn't be so tired and stressed."

I could feel my dander rising. We were teetering closer and closer to the precipice. *Going out* had become a household euphemism for everything disgusting Kirk did that I was too exhausted to bother speaking aloud.

"How does that make you feel, Kirk?" the therapist said. Did he ever say anything else? I couldn't believe you needed a PhD to ask people how they felt all day. "When Angie says you wouldn't be so tired if you didn't go out so much."

"I don't know. She knows I'm working on a big case right now," Kirk said. "Maybe the biggest in my career." *Big case* was another euphemism. I knew that the previous night he'd been out partying with his friends like he was still in his college fraternity, probably hitting up every strip club in all the land but who knew. When I did the laundry the next day, I could smell some other woman's cheap perfume on his clothes, the kind you buy at those stores in the mall that sell fake versions of the real thing. Often, I could smell a different women's perfume and I would ignore it, dumping his clothes into the washing machine.

"Right," I said, choking back tears. "The *big case*! Don't let me interfere with your *big case*!"

Mostly I was very cold and distant in those sessions. I don't know if it's the way humans adapt to any situation, or if it's my fear of being vulnerable, but I shut down. I adapted myself to Kirk's bad behavior, like I was one of those bugs that evolved to live in people's gas tanks. I had my friends. I had my activities. I had my kids; I filled my time, give or take. I smoked cigarettes and drank wine with a group of women on Jennifer's porch. Needing to fix my relationship was never on my radar. Did I know it was unfixable? Maybe, but I was paralyzed and felt my only choice was to keep my children in the same house with their father, which took precedence over how I actually felt about him or my personal happiness. It was my fault I picked him, and part of making amends for my broken picker was to stick it out for the kids until they graduated or even until they got married or had kids themselves. Maybe until I was on my deathbed. Regardless, I somehow convinced myself that our marriage was just a means to an end, full stop. It was a way to live and support my children. A vow I was meant to uphold.

In July of 2014, Emily and I were in Las Vegas for one of her many dance competitions. (Yes, I was also a dance mom at the time, which involved endless dance practices and out-of-state dance competitions.) I woke up one morning at the Bellagio to all these random texts on my phone. The content of said texts ranged from where to meet up to the agenda once said meetup occurred. The overall tone was sexual to the point of pornographic. I remember thinking, *That's weird. Did I leave my phone somewhere? Is someone playing a prank?* I couldn't put the pieces together. And then it hit me. Kirk had gotten a new phone—we had a family plan—and my phone was the main phone on the account. The way our family plan worked was that whoever was the keeper of the kingdom would get everyone's text messages unless that person activated the box in settings that kept their texts private. When Kirk got his new phone, he must have forgotten to tick that box, so I was getting all of his texts. And when I say all, I mean ALL.

I remember reading a particularly graphic text and looking out the window at the Strip and thinking, *Welp, this is it.*

It was five in the morning, and the sun was coming up, shimmering like it does in the desert. Like you're in a dream and James Gandolfini or Joe Pesci might emerge from the shimmer to whack you. At 5:01, I called Kirk and said, "Here's the deal. I'm not going to fight about it. I don't care. I'm not tracking your phone. But I'm taking it off the bill. I want you out of the house by the time we get home."

Meanwhile, I had to make it through the rest of Emily's dance competition. I didn't say a word about it to her the whole time. I didn't say a word to anybody there. I was in total shock but also in a state of resolved calm, eating chocolate-covered almonds and gummy bears out of the minibar by the fistful, not even caring that they probably cost eighteen hundred dollars. Finally, Emily and I flew home, and I told my sons, Luke and Sam, the next morning. They were shocked, which in retrospect was weird because their dad and I had barely said one word to each other for years, and he'd been sleeping in the guest room.

But as soon as I said, "Your father and I are getting a divorce," Luke started crying, so I started crying and Sam started crying then Emily started crying.

"Is there another woman?" Sam asked. He was fourteen years old; Emily was twelve, and Luke was nine. I think I said something like, "No . . . Not in the way that you're thinking . . . But your dad is an addict, and when he's in his addiction, he makes bad choices with other people who are also making bad choices."

And I just left it at that. Because what are you going to say? "Your dad and I are getting a divorce because he was stupid enough to sext on a family plan?"

But then Sam called Kirk and accused him of cheating on me, and Kirk didn't exactly deny it. I don't know what Kirk said because I wasn't in on that conversation, but it had to be brutal because Sam slept by my side for thirty days afterward. Sam was fourteen. It was the worst time for him to experience his parents getting a divorce, and I felt a lot of shame that I had somehow irreparably damaged my kids by not leaving Kirk earlier. Sometimes at night, I would imagine that I had never met Kirk, but I'd still somehow had Emily, Luke, and Sam, only with some other man who was a devoted father and husband. I even pictured myself back in the familiar well of the church, only a less churchy church, the kind where the preacher is a lesbian minister and I could turn to all of the sex workers who had ever been with Kirk and say, "Put down your suffering and start an a cappella choir with me."

The more my kids suffered, the more I wished that I had kicked Kirk to the curb when they were younger. But that's the thing about being a mom—the second your kids are born, you feel guilty. Even before that, while I was pregnant, I constantly worried I'd eaten the wrong thing or drank too much coffee or eaten the wrong cheese. Was I walking enough? Was I walking too much? Was I taking enough folic acid? Once the kids were born, was I reading them enough books? Were they the right books? Were they watching too much TV? Were their cell phones making them depressed? Was 5G giving them brain cancer? Was the COVID vaccine bad for them? Why didn't I limit their cell phone use? Why didn't I sign them up for more activities? Fewer activities? Why didn't I cook more nutritious meals? Why didn't I cook any meals period?

I wasn't a perfect person or a perfect mom. I made so many horrifying mistakes (especially in my addiction to pain pills, which I'll get into later). I was supposed to be my children's sole functioning parent and I got high for years. But perpetual guilt, I've learned, doesn't help my kids. It doesn't serve me.

I read an article recently about living from the top of the mind. Bill Crawford, the psychologist who wrote the article, basically talked about how shame and guilt fester in the lower part of our minds, like Gollum at the root of the Misty Mountains. These bottom-feeder emotions slither around in the fight-or-flight space rather than dwelling in what Crawford calls the "Top of the Mind," which is the neocortex, where we can make informed decisions based on events that actually happened. So, regret might serve a purpose to teach us how to make better choices going forward. Rather than feeling bad (shame and guilt) maybe it's more about shifting your perspective and saying, "That was then, but what is now? What next?" This exercise roots me in the present and helps me regain control over my vision for the future. Rather than staying locked on the mistakes I've made five, ten, twenty years ago, I can harness those feelings to make the right choices going forward.

These days, I also try to have compassion for Kirk. I don't want to go on a cruise with the man—I don't even want to

SHAME IS A MISERABLE LIFE PARTNER

have buffet brunch with him—but I have empathy for him. Okay, not a lot, but some. Okay, none. But we are both addicts. We're both recovering. In as much as anyone born in the seventies can change, I've changed. Every day, I keep making good choices. I choose my kids. I choose the podcast and Jennifer Welch. I choose myself.

PUMPS AND I JOIN THE FBI

~~~~~~~~~~~~~~~~

JEN

PUMPS CALLED MY LANDLINE at around 5:32 a.m. one Sunday, the Sunday that changed everything. We'd often call each other early in the morning to meet on our respective porches and have a phone cigarette together before our children woke up, so the savagely early hour didn't necessarily alarm me. When I saw the call, I expected to hear our customary phone-cigarette greeting: "Let's burn."

But instead, Pumps blurted, "Kirk didn't come home until 4:30 a.m. after the daddy-daughter dance at the country club."

Now, if you ask me, the whole concept of a daddy-daughter dance belongs in the same sexist bucket as the phrase "daddy's little girl." I consider both steppingstones to *Toddlers & Tiaras* and JonBenét Ramsey, and I wish our society would retire all these offensive phrases and customs as it has the phrases "master bedroom" and "spirit animal."

Anyway, Kirk and Emily had gone to said country club for the daddy-daughter dance in a limo—I know, limos for toddlers, also questionable—and then Kirk dropped Emily off at home around nine o'clock and zipped right out again in the limo.

"When I called Kirk at three in the morning, he called me back," Pumps informed me, speaking loudly into the phone. "But this morning, I got into his phone. There was no call log when I knew for a fact that I had called him. I was like, okay, that's weird."

I placed my coffee spoon on the counter and looked out the window into the side yard. I knew shit was about to get real, only at that moment, 5:34 a.m., I didn't exactly know *how* real. From how Pumps was breathing, I could tell she was pacing and smoking. "Everything was deleted. Outgoing calls, incoming calls, all the texts . . ." She trailed off. "What do you think that means?"

"Well, Pumps," I said. "He's probably hiding something. He probably screwed around. I mean, there's just no other explanation for it."

"I'll call you right back," she said and hung up. The day dawned blue and cloudless. During the brief pause that ensued, while I went to the front porch and smoked another cigarette, Pumps was interrogating Kirk about his call log, what happened to it, and why he'd deleted it.

At this point, two and a half years or so into my friendship with Pumps, Josh had just gotten out of rehab. The very first thing he'd done the day he got out was buy a beer. I still had PTSD about that. Pumps got it. Unlike a lot of other people who might have said, "Leave him!" or judged me for my choice not to, she could differentiate the addictive presence haunting my husband from the human being that was Josh Welch. I got her too.

Before I met Pumps, I remember asking Josh one night about Angie Olson—her married name—and Josh telling me how smart she was and how much I'd love her. He also told me that Kirk was the biggest pussy chaser on the planet. The word around town was that Kirk hosted golf tournaments where strippers blew the golfers right there on the green in the middle of the day. The man's vanity license plate read SPANKY. His license plate! SPANKY! It made me crazy to think about because I knew from my gay friends that their gyms would often padlock the steam room in the men's locker rooms to prevent hanky-panky, but these straight men could just have sex out in the open in the middle of their workday. The tricky thing was that I couldn't just drop, "Oh, hey, I heard your husband's the blowjob king of Action City" into my daily chitchat with Pumps. The right moment to divulge this information never presented itself, especially not at Chuck E. Cheese with our kids. The closer we got, ironically, the harder it got to say.

Sometime later that morning, I was brewing a second pot of coffee, when Pumps called me again. She told me Kirk tried to convince her he hadn't come home because—get this—he'd supposedly gone to IHOP with his buddies to grab breakfast. I knew right away this was a complete and utter lie.

"Maybe he really was at IHOP?" Pumps said. The plaintive timbre of her voice brought a lump to my throat.

"Then why did he delete everything from his phone?" I said. "Why delete your call logs if you're just chowing down on Thick 'N Fluffy French Toast?"

"I see what you mean," she said. "I'll call you right back."

While Pumps was off browbeating Kirk for a second time, I folded the laundry and got dressed. Twenty minutes later, Pumps called again.

"Let's burn," she said. I could hear her taking a deep drag on her cigarette, like a free diver preparing to go under for a long tête-à-tête with an octopus. "We've got to get to the bottom of this."

"Are you sure you want to open Pandora's box?" I said, staring at my neighbor's lawn. Pumps was terrified to take the next step, but she had chosen me, her grab-the-bull-by-the-horns friend. My mother always said that we subconsciously choose the right people to help us. She also told me there's a time to lie. This wasn't one of those times. Angie had no idea what a laughingstock her marriage was. The golf club information was widely known. But, again, I couldn't just say, "Hey, word on the streets is Kirk screws sex workers by the ninth hole."

Josh's first rehab in 2002 predated my introduction to Angie by about a year. I sat through Family Week, a confessional spew that some 1970s therapeutic menace decided was necessary for family members of addicts to endure publicly. I'd heard about every last beer. I'd heard every drunkalogue. It's hard to explain to somebody just how painful any of this is.

But I also understood Angie's desire to get the truth, because I'd also sought that truth with Josh.

"We have to get those phone records," I said. I had to help her. It felt like my calling. I could feel myself start to salivate.

The next day, Pumps showed up at my house. No matter how hard we tried, we couldn't break into Kirk's phone records. In 2007, your bill still came with a printed, itemized log of calls that listed who you called and how long you were on the phone, so your bill was as long and thick as a large-print version of *Moby-Dick*. We tried our best to hack our way in, but that didn't work. Pumps had a family plan, but Kirk's phone was connected to his law firm, so the paper version of Kirk's bill got mailed there. I called AT&T, impersonating Kirk's secretary, and trying my best to get those records, but all my best acting skills fell flat. Those operators were all sticklers. Angie was about to give up, but in an inspired "Last Chance Texaco" move, I decided we needed to drive to the AT&T store to see if we'd have better luck in person.

Now, you might be thinking, why even go to the AT&T store to get those records? You already know about the golf carts and the rug burns. You know about the deleted call log. Wasn't the suspicion enough to condemn this schmuck and GTFO? How much deeper down the rabbit hole do you need to go, sister? But there's something about getting to the heart of the truth when you're dealing with an addict. The intrigue revives you. It gives you a sense of control when you have none. The timelines and the details make you feel like you are doing something productive. Only your spouse isn't a Muppet. You can't ram your hand up their ass to move their mouth up and down to make them do and say what you want. But Pumps and I didn't fully grasp that yet. We thought, *Once we find this out, everything will fall into place.*

When we got to the AT&T store, Angie recognized Kirk's office manager driving out of the parking lot. As our two cars passed one another, she ducked her head.

"The office manager was here to make sure we couldn't get the fucking records," I said. "Kirk fucking sent him!"

"No way," Angie said. "Why would he do that?"

"Kirk is covering his ass. This is a seek-and-destroy mission, sis."

"Oh my God!" she said. "He *is* hiding everything!"

Angie was never reliable in these kinds of investigations; she always blew our cover, so I left her in the getaway car. Lightning flashed overhead, followed by thunder as I walked across the parking lot and into the store. As soon as I got inside, I scoped the scene for my target. About four or five blue-shirted representatives were milling around, one of whom was a young woman who looked like she could be susceptible to my act.

"Hey," I said, approaching her. "Can you help me out? I've got a little problem."

"What is it?" she said.

"I work for this guy," I said. "He's an attorney. He's just a complete asshole. He gave me some documents to shred, and he also gave me his AT&T bill, which I accidentally shredded. I was supposed to divide his personal calls from his work calls so that he could expense his work calls. I don't have access to the online account."

"I don't know . . ." she said. I could see how torn she was, but she didn't mention anything about Kirk's office manager, which was a huge relief. Maybe he hadn't got the records already.

For all you Gen Z readers, in 2007 people weren't totally paperless. Apple released the App Store in 2008. Folks were online, but they weren't chronically online the way they are now. Phone records weren't accessible online yet; you could only get a detailed billing via mail or the store. So, a physical printout of those records was the Golden Ticket, evidence-wise, of Kirk's shenanigans, the escorts he'd been calling, and all the numbers he'd deleted from his call log.

"I think my boss is going to fire me," I said, pretending to cry. "I'm a single mom, and I've got to pay for my kids' day care, and I really need this job for the health insurance."

"I'll print you those records," she said, then ran into the back of the store. I could hear the whine of the printer going and going. All I could think was, *We're going to get 'em. We're going to get 'em. We're going to get 'em.*

The nice woman handed me the phone records. I thanked her like she had saved my life, and maybe she had. The papers were still warm in my hand as I walked to my car where Pumps was waiting like a dog for its owner.

"I got 'em," I said, pulling my seat belt across my lap.

"I worship you," Angie said, high praise from a Christian. "I can't believe it. I can't believe that we got the records."

Pumps's world was falling apart (mine wasn't too far behind), but we were excited. Much later, Kirk would confirm that he had sent his office manager to try to get his phone records so he could see what he was up against, but the office manager had to wait until the next billing cycle. We got the records that day.

Next, we went to Staples. We got highlighters. We got paper clips, Post-it Notes, and binders and proceeded to my front porch. We had four months' worth of phone records and ten months' worth of cigarettes. We cross-referenced all the numbers on the call logs and started calling them. Pumps didn't yet know that the actual names of escort services and strip clubs don't appear on your phone bills. Instead made-up names would appear, to distract prying spouses. I zeroed in on all these fake-legit numbers, saying, "This is a strip bar. This is an escort service. Escort, escort, escort."

We called as many numbers as we could. Often women answered, and before we could get any juicy information, we wrote their numbers down on some poster board as if we were HUAC. I'd like to say it was a horrible time, and it was. Angie's marriage was a hundred percent over, and we both knew it. She had three young kids. My husband was sober, but barely. Neither Pumps nor I could say life was a picnic. But something about that investigation saved us, the purpose and determination of burning it all down. It took us out of ourselves.

The following Tuesday, we were at Angie's old house on Whippoorwill Road. I'll never forget it. We were smoking our faces off in her garage when she showed me a series of numbers she'd cross-checked and highlighted. She had this funny expression, somewhere between a grimace and a smile, like she was constipated.

"Kirk's gay," she said, like she had finally cracked the case. "And he's fucking our CPA. He has all these phone calls to him in April—from April first to fifteenth."

"Pumps," I said. "I think he's just doing your taxes. I mean, Kirk sucks, but this is a normal time to call your CPA." And then we just about died laughing. We laughed so hard that I nearly peed my pants, which just about happened to me every day since I had kids. But still, after Pumps and I calmed down, I put my phone on speaker and called a random number. When a woman answered, I took a deep, thoughtful drag off my Marlboro Light.

"Hi, my name is Angie Olson," I said. "I'm Kirk Olson's wife. I'm not mad at you, but my husband has a problem. I'm just trying to figure out if this man is worthy of me staying married to him, because I have three little kids, and I can get us out of this." Pumps stared at me with that frozen, constipated expression. The woman on the phone took a long pause. I could hear ice cubes clinking.

"He calls me all the time," she said finally. "He pays me for sex, and if I were married to him, I wouldn't want to be."

Angie's eyes widened. Finally, I recounted everything—the stuff I'd heard around town about the sex workers and the golf club. Funnily enough, Pumps admitted that she'd already gotten wind of these stories, but to make it through the day, she'd suppressed it all, pretending not to know. Angie had stopped having sex with Kirk long ago, so she'd managed to avoid any serious health risk, but still, the extent of the betrayal was staggering, especially hearing it enumerated call after call.

Angie and I spent countless hours FBI'ing the call log, either at her house or sitting on my front porch. One afternoon, I'd just put Roman down for his nap when we saw a series of fishy numbers. I don't recall why we thought they were fishy, but we did. I hit *67 to hide my ID and dialed the first number. Some guy answered. I sat there as he idiotically repeated, "Hello, hello?" while Angie diligently wrote down a description of his voice. I proceeded down the list, calling ten or twelve people, while Pumps took frantic notes on each person, like Carrie Mathison in *Homeland*.

Forty-five minutes later, we were still analyzing every individual voice and their level of collusion in this grand conspiracy. Suddenly, Kirk called. At this point, he knew we had found the phone records; Angie had no game and couldn't stop herself from telling him. She was the type of person who would declare her purchases going through customs.

"I was just in a meeting in my conference room," he said. "And everyone around the table just received an 'anonymous' call."

"Yeah? So?" Pumps said.

"I know it's you and Jennifer," Kirk said. "Whatever you're doing, please cut it out."

"No, it wasn't," Angie said, her voice high-pitched. "It wasn't us." No one, not even Bernie Madoff, had ever sounded more guilty.

"Please stop calling my colleagues. This is extremely embarrassing."

"Ha!" Angie said, so loudly I startled. Then she hung up and looked at me and we both started laughing; I thought I'd bust a gut. Angie laughed until she cried, then cried until her eyes turned puffy and swollen. "This is extremely embarrassing," she said, doing a spot-on impression of Kirk. Then we started laughing again even harder.

My husband, Josh, would relapse a couple more times after this. Kirk would also go to rehab repeatedly. Angie and I took turns shipping the crazy back and forth between ourselves like a game of hot potato. Simultaneously, we'd take the dogs to the vet, or our moms to the doctor, or our kids to toddler gymnastics. We'd throw our whole snot-nose brood into the Petri Dish and walk around Target together. And we'd go from laughing to crying and back again. Even in those dark days, finding out the worst thing, the worst betrayal, Pumps would look up at me, her face open as a door, and say, "Are we not fucking ridiculous? Let's burn." We'd fall over laughing like seventh graders.

Sometimes, we find our gifts in times of greatest duress, like pinecones in a forest fire, releasing seeds. These gifts only reveal themselves to us when the universe tests us so hard that we cry for mercy. Pumps and I both had to learn that life is two kinds of suffering, the kind the lazy Susan foists unfairly upon us and the kind we choose ourselves. At the center of all the pretending and tiptoeing and genuflecting, in the middle of all the lonely nights, wasn't another bottomless sinkhole but the promise of something better. The promise of something real and true. The promise of more. Maybe my greatest gift is spying. Maybe Pumps and I should have worked for the FBI, except she would blow our cover, and I hate everything about guns.

LET ME SPEAK TO THE MANAGER

ANGIE

RACIST KARENS DESERVE THE weight of the entire world's ire. As do the Karens who refuse to bake wedding cakes for same-sex marriages. But the subsection of Karens, the I-want-to-talk-to-the-manager Karens, that vertical deserves another review.

Why? Because sometimes the steak is overcooked, and someone's got to send it back. Sometimes, the service is slow. The queso isn't hot enough, or the coffee doesn't have enough pumpkin spice. Or it has too much pumpkin spice. Sometimes the line for the Delta Sky Club is too long. When I'm at a restaurant and it takes the server forever to bring extra ketchup or the bill, I go speak to the hostess, but in a polite way. I don't leave negative Yelp reviews, even when I have a subpar experience. Sometimes, *somebody* needs to talk to the manager. Sometimes, you need a Karen like me to stick up for your wimpy ass.

Again, as long as you aren't being a total asshole or saying anything racist, homophobic, or overtly offensive, you have a right to stand up for yourself and your steak, which should always be medium rare. Recently, Jennifer and I were doing one of our live podcasts in Los Angeles. She started telling the story about my ex-husband Kirk's sexcapades the night of the daddy-daughter dance. The audience was in stitches—who wouldn't be?—when I realized it was possible we had both been FBI Karens. Jen will be upset when she reads this because she does *not* want to equate herself with a Karen. She likes to think of herself as cooler/MILF-ier/more with-it than I am, but the reality is, we PI-Karen'ed.

But two events happened the week of the daddy-daughter dance that were peak Karen. Again, Jennifer was involved in both, and I believe that her participation made her a Karen by association, but she would never admit it, even in a court of law.

You might be thinking, *What the fuck is a daddy-daughter dance? And Why does this princess-y, retrograde, Oedipal moment still exist in the year 2024?* But let's move beyond that very reasonable query for a second. I'm not sure if I gave too much thought to the daddy-daughter dance, good or bad, or even its symbolism. The one thing on my mind was why did Kirk need to rent a limo? I got that he was escorting our daughter, Emily, his "date,"—I know, *ew*—and that this gesture was meant to mark the passage from Emily's little girlhood to her little ladyhood debut. But then Kirk rented a limo—I know, questionable—went to the dance, then took our daughter home, sped off in said limo and did not return until he stumbled into the kitchen the following morning. The TLDR: I would later learn that on this night of debauchery during which I couldn't get a hold of him for trying, Kirk likely schtupped multiple sex workers.

How did I discover all of this? Did Kirk confess it all in a projectile burst of conscience? No. Did he admit it to me in a moment of moral clarity? Also, no. Jennifer and I conducted a thorough, multipronged FBI-style investigation into the events of that night. The investigation took place over several days. It felt like finals week at college, the part where you're up at four in the morning, trying to memorize Russian history from the tzars to Gorbachev, and all you've eaten are Twizzlers. I didn't shower or sleep for more than fifteen-minute intervals. I mainlined coffee and possibly snorted an energy drink. Maybe it was exhaustion or pride, but at some point, I decided it would be a good idea to interrogate our couple's counselor to find out if he had any information, something Kirk had confessed during a private session.

I'd written down all my points and questions on a yellow legal pad—my evidence of all of his transgressions. Of course, I knew the reality of the situation—I was in denial, but I wasn't a total idiot—but I still thought our therapist/counselor could turn it all around and tell me, "All of this is a figment. Your husband has been secretly taking conga lessons to surprise you for your anniversary!"

But instead of scheduling an appointment with the extremely mediocre therapist who Kirk and I had seen for almost two decades, Jen and I drove to his office and staked him out. At the time, it seemed prudent, like the next right action, interrogating the guy with the most intel in the parking lot of his office. The minute the man innocently pulled into his usual space, I leaped from the car on the attack, like a . . . well, like a Karen, speaking to the manager about some perceived injustice. He seemed taken aback. Why was I standing there, in my mismatched, droopy athleisure, clutching a legal pad and yelling at him about Kirk when I'd sullenly sat through years of couple's therapy saying nothing and acting like an ambivalent teenager? I started accosting him with my barrage of personal questions as he stood there, clutching his YETI.

"Is Kirk getting BJs and doing toot-toot in the champagne room at Bare Assets while I'm driving everyone to soccer? Is he having threesomes with women named ManDee and Clitorissa? Am I too old to get married again?" Then I think I told our therapist I could sue him.

"Do you want to schedule an appointment?" he asked finally.

"Not really, no," I said, defeated. I turned to Jennifer and gave her a nod. My heart was pounding. I felt like I was in *To Die For*, and it was all about to go down. Looking back, I don't know what I expected our therapist to tell me. That Kirk *hadn't* fucked a bunch of other women? That he was secretly a cult leader or running an MLM? Maybe he was in WITSEC and the strippers were his cover? Maybe our mediocre therapist would offer to marry me and take me away from all this?

I read more evidence at him from the legal pad, the same story that had been playing in my head on endless loop: the dance, the deleted numbers, the FBI investigation.

"Let's schedule an appointment," he repeated. "I have time the day after tomorrow in the late morning." I have to hand it to him: He refused to feed into my crazy, which was both frustrating and soothing. I couldn't help but feel that he was somehow in on it, in on everything. At the bachelor parties. In the limo. Regardless, I made an appointment. At said subsequent session, my last session with him, which Kirk also attended, he actually handed us a copy of the book *After the Affair: Healing the Pain and Rebuilding Trust When a Partner Has Been Unfaithful*. I knew, looking at that white-and-pink ombre cover, that Ol' Shrinky Dink just didn't get it. In as much as the word *normal* means anything, he was used to normal-people marital problems, the kind where rekindling trust after an infidelity was even possible. The kind where the therapist hands a couple a book and they both read it. Maybe they would even hold each other and weep. The man who cheated on his wife one time might look at his wife and say, "I love you and I will do anything to win back your trust." But as soon as I saw the book, I laughed in Kirk's face and asked for a refund.

After climbing back in Jen's Land Rover that day, I felt demoralized. Not because the couple's counselor hadn't let me in on all Kirk's dirty secrets, but because now the onus was on me to admit I already knew the answer. What did I want him to say? "Girl, don't tell Kirk, but he's got a core wound the size of Texas, no wonder he banged every woman with fake titties from here to Tulsa. It wasn't anything you did or didn't do. No amount of vajayjay will ever heal his broken wiener."

The real problem—okay, there were a lot of problems—the *current* problem was that if the investigation stopped, it meant my regular life resumed, and if my regular life resumed, then I had to face the truth, which was that I'd married a man who'd piss on my leg and tell me it was raining. I'd done that. Me. I'd married a rampant sex addict and liar. A word about sex addiction: It's a disease like alcohol and drug addiction. In Kirk's case, his addiction centered on the transactional nature of the sex rather than engaging in a string of extramarital romantic relationships. I think sex addiction is more frowned upon than drug or alcohol addiction partly because of the moral implications, but it's still just another way to get high. It often affects people with mood disorders and other mental health conditions that go back to childhood. I often struggled to understand how anyone could find the time to rail *so many sex workers* when I could barely give myself a moisturizing hair mask. It took me a long time to wrap my head around how the sneaking around and the lying also got him high. The procurement was likely as much of a turn-on as the actual sex. I'm not castigating the guy for his darn issues. I'm saying that the situation became completely untenable for me, and it was time to send my damn steak back, possibly to the butcher. Maybe even to the cow.

"Well, that didn't work," I said, looking at Jennifer. I could have been talking about accosting my soon-to-be ex-therapist or my soon-to-be ex actual life.

"Pumps," Jen said. Her eyes were getting that weird gleam that meant *I have an insane idea.* "We need to go up to IHOP and ask the hostess or the manager if they remember whether a limo full of guys pulled up to eat there at three in the morning. They're going to remember that. Any employee's got to remember that. They don't get adult men pulling up in a limo at 3 a.m."

We look at each other across the center console and then I called the IHOP and asked to SPEAK TO THE MANAGER—or whomever was on duty on Saturday night. The teenager who answered the phone told me to come by at four o'clock; somebody from the night shift would be there.

Weirdly, Kirk called at the exact moment when Jennifer and I were deciding what to do next. Right away, he started talking about IHOP, blathering a bunch of nonsense. It was like he knew we were talking about him.

"What'd you order?" I said, doing my best impression of Detective Olivia Benson.

"Thick 'N Fluffy French Toast," he said.

"Thick 'N Fluffy French Toast," I echoed as Jen wrote down Kirk's order on the legal pad. "That's interesting. You didn't order a side of bacon? You always order an extra side of bacon . . ."

"Oh, that's right, I did," he said. *Bacon,* Jennifer wrote.

"I'm going up there to meet the manager, so I'll find out for myself!" I announced, hanging up. Jennifer started whacking me with the legal pad. Now Kirk was going to bribe that manager to tell us he'd been to IHOP. Of course, that's exactly what happened. Kirk bribed the IHOP manager to say he remembered Kirk and his friends pulling up in a limo and ordering Thick 'N Fluffy French Toast and

Colorado Omelettes. The alibi was very detailed, down to the over-easy eggs. So, when I marched into that IHOP and demanded to SPEAK TO THE GODDAMN MANAGER RIGHT NOW, in my best and loudest Karen voice, the manager insisted Kirk and his friends had been there. No matter how many times I insisted he hadn't. No matter how hard I grilled him for holes in the story.

My Karen'ing had met its goddamn match: the Brotherhood of Man.

Now, if you don't know what the Brotherhood of Man is, you are likely a member or benefitting from it, but it's basically the cabal of white, straight men who run the world, all of them in an endless circle jerk, patting each other on the back, standing up and lying for each other. The same men who tell me to relax when I have a perfectly good goddamn reason to be anything but. The ones who elected Trump. The ones I worshipped and made out with when I was a Kappa Kappa Gamma while I was barfing my guts out after a kegger. This was how the white boys got the jobs, the big houses. This was how they kept accruing generational wealth. It was how they got elected president for a second term even when they were relentlessly moronic and four-times-indicted. That's how powerful the Brotherhood is! You can refuse to blend your self-tanner and half the country still votes for you!

There was a huge part of me that kept praying the night of the daddy-daughter dance was a one-off. A veritable orgy that you write off as a pancake breakfast. For most people, the daddy-daughter dance alone would have been devastating. But for me, that would have been the biggest gift on the planet because it meant my marriage could have recovered. I could have bought myself a copy of *After the Affair* and read it cover to cover. I could have healed the pain. I could have rebuilt trust. It would've been the biggest win if it had all just ended there. But throwing a book at the problem was going to do as much good as an umbrella in a hurricane.

Even with all the evidence mounting against my marriage, I refused to Karen it directly. I would Karen my therapy sessions, the IHOP manager, even the author of *After the Affair*. But I wouldn't Karen my actual life. I wouldn't send it back for a different order or demand to see the manager who was none other than—you guessed it—me. I don't think I talked to my therapist about *myself* that whole time; all I did was complain ceaselessly about Kirk. It took me so long to realize that the only way to heal myself was to focus on my actual self.

The thing about Karen'ing—not racist Karen'ing, but *pushy* Karen'ing, one of those Karens who screams "REPRESEN-TATIVE!" into the phone until someone from a far-flung click-farm gets on the line and transfers you to a supervisor, is that I feel like the term has also become a sexist was of say-ing "older woman I would no longer like to fuck but who is nonetheless making a valid complaint I am not brave enough to make on my own." Yes, if Jesus were alive, He would prob-ably stay on the line and take the customer satisfaction survey at the end of the call. He could heal the unhelpful bot who doesn't give a flying frog's fat ass about His day. He would not send back His queso when it's too cold, even though cold queso is the devil's work and should be banned in fifty states, or at least in Texas and Oklahoma. Meanwhile, men can be assertive assholes six ways from Sunday, and nobody gives a holy hoot.

Jennifer and I have a running joke that we should run a side hustle called Husband Busters where we Cagney-and-Lacey people's cheating spouses for them. We would make a mint, trust me. But the truth was, my problems went so much deeper than Kirk's lies. It was about my deeply rooted need to have everything be picture-perfect. Just one dalliance. A good hair day. Two cars in the driveway. It was about my own willful blindness and my inability to let go and summon my inner freaking Karen.

YOUR MIND IS YOUR OWN DAMN BUSINESS

~~~~~~~~

JEN

THE NIGHT MY HUSBAND, Josh, and I met at Flip's Wine Bar in OKC, I wasn't expecting to find my soulmate. I don't believe in soulmates or twin flames. Pragmatism reigns supreme in my brain. But even if I did believe in the concept of soulmates, I did *not* think I'd ever, in a million years, find mine at Flip's, the nineties-style Italian bistro and bar where Josh was a fixture during happy hour. He hung out with a group of swinging-dick young professionals whose primary purpose was to get tanked and hit on anything with a pulse that wasn't nailed to the floor. I realize this may seem somewhat unsavory in this current age, but he and his crew were not without a certain charm.

"Can I get you a drink?" Josh said, indicating the array of illuminated bottles behind the bar.

I'd like to say that the moment we met was like that scene in *West Side Story* when Maria and Tony met at the dance in the gym. They gazed deeply into each other's eyes and danced a romantic pas de deux like they were the only people in the universe. Well, that didn't happen. Instead, Josh launched into a rant on what I would later learn were His Topics: religion (bad), Republicans (worse), and the death penalty (don't get him fucking started, sister).

Initially, I liked Josh well enough, though I wasn't attracted to him. I thought he was smart and fun. I'd been spending most of my free time going to clubs with my gay male friends, most of whom I met slinging margaritas and loaded boneless wings at Chili's in my twenties. Part of the reason I socially gravitated toward gay boys was that many of them didn't fit into the religious social scene. They'd been betrayed by their families and had to think beyond the black-and-white biblical worldview. Even though I was straight and a cheerleader in high school and all that other supposedly essential social nonsense, I always felt like there was a membrane between me and the rest of the world. Maybe it was because of my secular proclivities, but I never felt seen. Three bites into an enchilada at dinner, someone would start saying grace, trying to save me, or getting me to "pray on it."

Josh was straight too, that much was obvious. He loved fashion and shopping and he liked to make out with women. The idea that someone shared my reality-based worldview and that this someone could be a heterosexual man from Hugo, Oklahoma, a town of five thousand people, most of whom were Evangelicals, was surprising to say the least. It piqued my interest.

Over the course of several months, Josh pursued me relentlessly. He often came to pick me up from my design studio in his forest green Lexus SUV with a fresh pack of Marlboro Lights waiting for me in the cup holder. We would drive around Oklahoma City's historic neighborhoods, talking for hours. Initially, I was hesitant because Josh presented as a womanizer at the bar. However, those long drives revealed a man with more depth and curiosity than I had ever imagined. Yes, he was charming and could spin a great yarn, but he was also thoughtful and caring, not to mention liberal. We were able to have deep, meaningful conversations about existentialism, politics and music, our minds pinging from one topic to the next. That intellectual connection was intoxicating for me. So many people in my high school had this extra "passenger" in their life, a holy chaperone watching their every move from the sidelines. With Josh, it was just the two of us. I wasn't used to experiencing this on other dates and just assumed part of dating was feeling some level of disconnect, always looking out the window and imagining the real version of the conversation I would have later with one of my gay friends.

But Josh and I talked about everything in that car. He wanted to get serious right from the beginning, but I friend-zoned him for a few months. One late afternoon, we were out by the Museum of Art, when he said, "I can't wait until you turn the corner on me." The sun was setting against the pink low-hanging clouds, and it stirred something romantic in me, but I still fought against falling for him. Then we went out on a long drive somewhere in the sticks. Josh wept as he spoke about his early childhood in rural Oklahoma. His family was progressive, but incredibly broken. His mother struggled with addiction and debilitating depression. She lived through a suicide attempt. His father had all the isms.

Josh had bought his half-brother, Matt, a new car and put a stereo in it for him. He was so proud of being able to buy Matt that car. That same summer, Matt, who was sober at the time, got in a car wreck and died. Josh was devastated. I found more depth and honesty in what Josh said about the cruel absurdity of Matt's death than some white-picket-fence, straight-down-the-fairway version of reality. He saw the world with a startling clarity. He revealed his emotions. I guess I was attracted to that. I was attracted to the truth.

Josh never tried to mask the ugly parts of his childhood. There was a brutal honesty and vulnerability about the unfiltered way he described his upbringing. It made me feel closer to him than I'd ever felt with any boy or man I'd ever known. My father had never shared his real feelings. My previous Oklahoma boyfriends had kept their emotions under wraps out of some sense of macho-cowboy bullshit. But Josh told me everything and I returned the favor. He made me laugh and cry and he made me feel alive.

After a while, we clung to each other like ticks on a dog. We believed in evolution and science and—wait for it—dinosaurs. We believed in abortion, gay marriage, and trans rights. We didn't care one iota about joining a church or, frankly, any church at all. We never even talked about church or even said the word *prayer* except when Josh sang along to the song "Save a Prayer" by Duran Duran on the radio.

At twenty-seven years old, I thought I had the whole system of life beat. But what I didn't know, as I watched the man who would become my husband and the father of my children down shot after shot at Flip's Wine Bar, was that Josh had been drinking since he was a young boy. That he drank like it was his hobby, his passion, and his full-time job. Of course, later, I noticed everything we did revolved around easy access to alcohol. But like all women in the throes of catching feelings, I thought I could change him. I thought Josh's partying would decrease over time as he settled into the comforts and confines of our once-in-a-lifetime love. I thought wrong.

A year after Josh and I met, I noticed my period was late, and my boobs felt tender, which could only mean one thing. I went to CVS to buy a pregnancy test. Later that night, I emerged from the bathroom with the pee-soaked stick to find Josh in the kitchen, popping the top off his fourth beer of the night.

"I'm knocked up," I announced.

"Oh shit," he said, placing the bottle gingerly on the counter. In case you were wondering, he didn't pick me up and gleefully spin me around or drop to his knees and press his face into my stomach. Instead, we looked at each other, terrified. Like I had just told him aliens were about to invade the planet and he had five minutes to gather his favorite possessions, procure a truck and a generator and meet me outside. Thoughts flicked through my head. Would Josh be able to cut down on the partying? Would being a dad change him? Was I ready to be a mom? I was twenty-eight years old. Could I be a mother and run my burgeoning design business? Would I ever see my friends again if I ceased to be fun? What kind of parents would we be? Were we even ready? Is anyone ready?

As the weeks wore on, we discussed getting hitched but decided to wait because I didn't want to have a big belly or cankles at my wedding. Obviously, my decision to be an unwed mother probably caused chatter, but I was too vain to care about the vultures. After Josh's rehab stints plus our divorce, it seems laughable now that my main imperative was to look model-hot in my wedding dress. But I wanted the intake of breath when the door opened, and all the heads turned toward me standing there—a picture-perfect reveal.

Josh and I moved in together without getting married, which likely raised some eyebrows in Nichols Hills, an affluent neighborhood in Oklahoma City. Even if my marital status—or lack thereof—kick-started a ripple in the gossip chain, I remained unaware. My friend group consisted of mostly gay guys who didn't judge me, plus a sprinkling of progressive women whose panties didn't get in a bunch over a piece of paper that allowed us to file joint tax returns.

Again, we shacked up before everything went down, so Josh was still a high-profile attorney. I was an up-and-coming interior designer, going out into the world trying to put my flag down in the form of window dressing and upholstered ottomans. Nichols Hills is a small neighborhood. Everyone's in everybody's business like they're watching your life unfold on reality TV, an experience that is not abstract to me, thanks to being on *Sweet Home Oklahoma*. I'd never even wanted to be on reality TV, not that I have anything against it, but when the casting agency approached me, I felt I couldn't say no. The show brought a lot of national attention to my design business, so it was invaluable in that regard. We've all read and heard that many reality shows are edited to be more interesting than real life, which we all know is mostly a lot of laundry and making dinner. To remedy this, some TV producers try to get cast members into situations of maximum conflict and, sometimes, maximum alcohol consumption.

From the beginning, our production company knew Pumps, Lee (our other costar), and I refused to have conflict while filming. The word *drama* is overused in popular parlance to the point of meaninglessness, but we didn't want to catfight or represent women as vehicles of negativity. This was our main stipulation. Did this affect the ratings of the show? Who can say. Sometimes Lee would sleep over at my house, or we stalked Pumps at her house because if it weren't for her kids' activities, she was mostly a homebody. But the three of us were all great friends who got along, so our show wasn't the usual salacious, table-flipping Housewives fare. By the way, I respect the hell out of those shows. They are extremely fun and entertaining, but Pumps, Lee, and I really wanted our show to represent female friendship. Lee was divorced and a single mom, running a business. Pumps spoke truthfully about having to downsize her house. I was very honest about Josh's various issues.

Maybe the problem, at least in TV terms, was that the three of us didn't demonstrate enough friction. Our inner conflict stayed hidden, like bed bugs at a fancy hotel. We agreed on everything. We hit our marks. We laughed. Our dogs were cute.

I could handle being on reality TV, in part, because I ultimately didn't care what people thought about me. I'd cultivated this mindset from a young age, first as a survival tactic growing up a liberal atheist in red-state Oklahoma, and later because it just made good sense. I knew if I was constantly concerned about how my neighbors were judging me, I'd live in a state of constant fear, a seventh-grade lunchroom eat-or-be-eaten mentality. I remember when I was in in junior high, a bunch of girls randomly decided to turn on me because I didn't wear much makeup. Moments like that can be devastating when you're a teenager. Your world is small, and these sudden shifts can feel seismic. Why was my lack of makeup so important to them? I went home and cried to my mother. Why do we care so much about our place in the pecking order and why does it all return to an endless riptide of these humiliating childhood moments? But anyone who judges me for my life choices now is certainly not worth an iota of my time.

This goes both ways. Whether my neighbor is married, divorced, poly, screwing Brad Pitt or Mariska Hargitay is none of my fucking business. (Though if they are screwing

Brad Pitt, I do have some questions.) It's so easy to stick your nose in someone else's life and be an armchair anchor-woman, sounding off on what you think is wrong, right, or in between. We ceaselessly scroll our social media feeds—your high school boyfriend's fiancée, your cousin, that guy you met at that bachelorette party years ago before your tits sank—thinking we know what's going on in their lives. We judge. We comment. Some of us slide into DMs. But the truth is, what with filters and contour makeup and AI, nobody knows the real story. No one knows the difficulty and pain that is going on in anyone's actual life. No one knows about how I wept on the sofa over what those girls said about my lack of makeup. No one knows I cried, except my mom, who smoothed my hair out of my face and told me it was going to be okay.

So, when the morality chorus started spilling that sweet, sweet tea about Josh and me moving in together before we were married, or when total strangers comment-dump about my looks online, I mostly don't care. Mostly. I know I'm a public figure, and for some reason, it's part of my job as a podcaster to have a bunch of lookie-loos in their pajamas tell me I'm ugly and over-the-hill. But, technically, just as my lipstick and love life aren't anyone's business, their comments and opinions on my opinions aren't *my* business. I know, easier said than done. But everything that goes on between other people's ears doesn't belong between mine. I tell my kids: What other people think about you is none of your business. Your mind is your own business.

This idea may sound simple, but I remember I was at my therapist's office some years ago, giving her the usual spiel. I was telling her about how I'd broken into the rented duplex where Josh had temporarily hitched his wagon after he got out of rehab. Why? So I could search his bathroom for any contraband pills. Nothing had ever felt more important to me than this deranged quest.

"Why does he have thirty pills when he just got out of rehab? Why does he have controlled substances at all?" I asked her, like she was the jury, and I was Annalise Keating in *How to Get Away with Murder*. "He's getting high again. He's picking drugs over me and the kids. Josh's father encouraged drinking, gifting Josh Corona in his Easter basket when he was still a little kid." After finishing my *Jerry Springer* monologue, my therapist paused, looked right at me, and said, "Jennifer, why did you pick him?"

The skin on my breastbone tightened. Was my therapist suggesting that I was the problem? It was so much easier for me to shine the light on somebody else's dysfunction than to study my own business. Maybe I'd picked a broken person to distract me from my own brokenness. Looking back, I was just as sick and suffering as Josh was. I just wasn't taking drugs. Her question hit me like a dodgeball in the gut and I sat there, stymied. Why did I pick him? Was the question the answer? When you're with an addict, you lose sight of the person they are minus their addictions, but more than that, you lose sight of the person *you* were before codependence ruled your life. It's like a window in a rental apartment, painted over so many times that it no longer opens. I knew it was a good question, but I couldn't answer her. In a way, this book is my answer.

But the truth was, Josh was my choice. I picked that man, stayed with him, and spent years talking about him and at him and trying my darnedest to fix him. But the thing is, I couldn't fix him because—get this—no one can fix anyone. We can only fix ourselves and even that is a full-time job. I practically had to call in the cavalry. When I let go of the desire to fix and control everything, this unclenching seeped into every other aspect of my life. I quit drinking and smoking. I started to put myself and my own issues and needs first. I fixed myself and eventually it saved my marriage.

It took a while for Josh to get clean. So long, I had to divorce him, but that wasn't the end of our story. We're to-gether now, *legally* divorced but married by common law—and thriving. We wear rings and all that meaningless public hogwash. Now that he's in recovery, he's a devout father to our two sons and a kind, loving partner to me. I tell people I divorced Josh, the addict. But I *live* with Josh, my husband, and the father of my two boys. I finally know that while his sobriety affects me, it has nothing to do with me. I could have the mind of Barack Obama, the body of Gisele Bünd-chen, and the temperament of Florence Nightingale, and I still couldn't change him. Whether Josh picks up a drink or a drug has nothing to do with whether I sneeze or look at him cross-eyed. At the end of the day, we can be there for each other, but still remain independent.

I'm sure people think it's crazy as hell that I took Josh back. Or they don't believe he's the man I know him to be in my very soul. The man I knew he was on those long drives, as the sun set over the wide horizon. Honestly, I don't care either way. After all, it's none of my business.

FAMILY WEEK

ANGIE

WHEN GENERAL WILLIAM TECUMSEH Sherman said, "War is hell," he'd obviously never experienced Family Week at Pine Grove in Hattiesburg, Mississippi. I agree, it must have been uncomfortable for those Union soldiers to get their legs amputated without anesthetic and only a dirty stick or a piece of leather to bite into, but did those soldiers have to sit there, with a bunch of weeping spouses and family members, while the pain and failure of their relationships were dredged up in a therapeutic group setting?

The first time Kirk was in rehab for sex addiction I flew down to Mississippi for Family Week, having no idea what to expect beyond what Jennifer had told me, so I knew it wasn't going to be a party. Still, I couldn't breathe. I was emaciated. My hair was falling out in chunks when I washed it like I was on chemo.

The hotel was in this tiny town, and the only place to get food within walking distance was the gas station. I hadn't eaten for two days, and I was starving. I got one of those sandwiches in a plastic box. I'd reserved a rental car, but the Hertz was somehow out of cars when I got there, so I was walking back from the gas station along the highway with my little sandwich, wondering, *How did my life get here? How did this happen? Why am I walking along the highway in Mississippi with this motherfucking sandwich?*

The next morning, I woke up and attended a group therapy session where all the addicts, including Kirk, described their indiscretions in vivid, overly graphic detail. Remember when you got a stomach virus as a kid? You projectile vomited all over your bedroom or the bathroom. Anywhere else besides the toilet or the throw-up bowl. Afterward, you felt so much better. Well, you know who didn't feel better? Your mom. She had to clean everything up. As someone who had been a kid and was now a mother, I knew what it was like to be in both roles.

I just remember thinking, *My mother did not raise me to sit in a room with a popcorn ceiling to listen to people reveal their private problems like they were discussing what movie to see.* One family member was a school counselor, and her husband told a story about how he spent the whole day on the computer, masturbating on camera. Some of the people were addicted to sex workers, and I'd swap glances with their family members across the room like, "I see you, girl." There were people who had been having multiple affairs. A seventy-five-year-old grandpa fucking a blowup doll in his wife's underwear. You get the picture.

Then Kirk got up there and said that he had been bumping uglies with sex workers since he was in his teens. He thought about escorts and porn all the time. His mind was a blur, thinking about how many times he could pay to do the no-pants dance with strangers before dinner. Look, I get it. I love junk food. But you'd never catch me sneaking out to the Kum & Go in the middle of the night to buy a box of Little Debbie Moon Pies. What's more, the man had dropped around hundreds of thousands of dollars on this penchant of his since we got married. He'd been spending more money than Midas on sex workers and drugs! In case you think we were rich or that's how much money we were liquid, we absolutely were not. The man had been secretly draining our personal finances to pay for his sizable sex habit. The fact that I never noticed this was happening is a whole other book about the power of denial, but Kirk kept writing himself checks every month until our six-thousand-square-foot house went into foreclosure, and we ended up deadass broke. At the time, I wasn't working; I'd quit the law firm to be a stay-at-home mom when I started having kids, so I didn't have anything to fall back on. If it weren't for my parents, my kids and I would have wound up homeless.

The roots of Kirk's addiction, I learned, weren't just a flaw in his libido. Turned out, his uncle and mentor, who was a big lawyer in Oklahoma City, had been doing the same exact thing. What's more, he'd trained Kirk how to do it. When Kirk was in high school and college, he mowed yards as a summer job. His uncle ran his house like a brothel, and when

Kirk would mow his uncle's lawn, he'd see women coming and going and who knows what else. Was this where the disconnect originated? Or was it even earlier, with his parents? Regardless, it all came out during Family Week. Kirk told me (and by me, I mean me and everyone else sitting in the group therapy circle at Family Week), "I've been spending all our money. This is a problem I've had since I was a kid. I've been fucking multiple sex workers. I think about having sex with them all day. I'm always communicating with at least seven of them at a time and I don't know if I'll ever be able to stop."

Nothing, I mean nothing was worse than being in that room in Hattiesburg, Mississippi, listening to my ex-husband deliver a monologue about everything—the women, the drugs, the lying and the sneaking around. The sheer amount of vaginas he was sticking his penis into made my skin crawl and my stomach contract. I was only able to make it about eight minutes into his confession before I had to run out and puke.

Later that night, after *also* having explosive diarrhea, I knelt by my bed and tried to pray. "Please put the pieces of the glass house back together. Don't let my kids have to grow up in this spinning carousel of lies. Please keep my life intact. I'll never fuck Kirk or touch so much as a hair on his head. I will force him to sleep in the guestroom and make him wash his own underpants and sheets, but please make us a family again."

Granted, all prayers are naive, but this lament was almost too pathetic to include in this book. It makes me swoon with mortification to type it. Not just that I was still hoping for the whole situation to magically disappear, but that I didn't have the wherewithal to understand that the Kirk I thought I knew never existed in the first place. That fact broke me. I thought I was living this life that I never actually lived.

I remember something Jennifer said to me around this time: "It's kind of like there's two movies going on. There's the movie that you watch when he's with you, and then he walks out the door. And this whole other movie plays. You would never think it was the same person. But you've got to reconcile those two people to find the truth."

Later, in 2009, Jennifer and I were on a girls' trip in Mexico when Tiger Woods's predilection for cheating put the spotlight on sex addiction. His wife allegedly found shady messages on Tiger's phone and then chased him out of the house with a golf club. During the press conference, Tiger Woods announced he was going away for treatment.

I looked at Jennifer, and I said, "I guarantee you he's going where Kirk went, and Kirk's going to tell every single person in Oklahoma City," which was exactly what happened; Kirk couldn't contain himself. He couldn't wait to tell everybody that he and Tiger Woods had gone to the same treatment center. He wasn't even embarrassed. They hadn't been there at the same time, but Kirk loved the fact that he and Tiger Woods had maybe done art or music therapy at the same place.

Despite everything, despite Kirk's apparent willingness to put my health and our family at risk, I was still reluctant to let go of the facade. I wanted my children to have two parents who lived together, even if the last time we'd been intimate was during the Obama administration. I even told myself, *This is going to pass. It will all get better. Kirk has just got to get through sex rehab and go to SLAA (Sex and Love Addicts Anonymous), and then I'll be able to keep my family together.*

When I finally summoned the courage to let go, the pain was indescribable. I felt like I was walking through fire, and I feared it would haunt me forever. But then one morning, I woke up and brushed my teeth. I looked over at the other his-and-hers sink where Kirk used to brush his teeth. He wasn't there. I was alone and I felt nothing. His absence no longer cast a dark shadow over my life. My resentment no longer sat on my chest like an anvil. And I took a shallow breath and let it out before going downstairs and fixing myself a quadruple espresso and a huge plate of eggs. And grits.

PRAY THE GAY TO STAY

JEN

NOTHING STICKS IN MY craw more than half-assed, cherry-picked allyship. For instance, if I go to a party thrown by a close friend—who happens to be gay—and everyone in the neighborhood shows up to get their IG snap. Meanwhile, I know for a fact that some of those same ass-lickers vote straight red down the ticket, even though that vote means the potential elimination of gay marriage or other discrimination protections. I've always found this hypocrisy breathtaking.

Some of the private schools in our area require kids and parents to sign a morality pledge affirming that no one in their home is "homosexual" or a drug user (as if these two were somehow synonymous). I cannot fathom how any person, let alone a parent, could sign a document that dehumanizes and shames an entire community, especially a community meant to support and nurture young people. In full transparency, Angie sent her kids to one of these schools. I often called her out on how she could send them to a school where a clause

like that is part of the culture. I would point out the irony
of that clause, how it was actually "unchristian" and anti-
intellectual. For instance, the binaries of gay and straight were
actually nineteenth- and twentieth-century coinages. Plato
slept with guys. So did Shakespeare. Some of his sonnets were
addressed to men. A recent documentary revealed how Abraham Lincoln pursued relationships with four different men,
which the filmmakers asserted was more common during his
lifetime than you might think. Yes, that's right. Honest Abe
had boyfriends. The world is gay. Get over it.

"Oh, I just ignore that part," she said, adding, "Kirk signs
the damn thing anyway."

Later, Angie would tell me that it was one of her biggest regrets that she sent her children to that school, that the
meaning and intent of the "morality clause" reverberated in
her heart at pickup and drop-off and when she watched her
daughter, Emily, at cheer.

When Angie's biological father died, it was a big wake-
up call for her, the way these big losses can be. I remember
her telling me, "I don't believe in heaven anymore. I don't
believe in an afterlife. I don't believe in the Bible." I was so
shocked because those are obviously core tenets of the Evangelical faith. To decry them meant something major. This
was around the same time that her political views were shifting and she started consuming news on MSNBC nonstop. I
mean, I couldn't get that woman to attend a ballet or come
with me to a museum, but these days Pumps is a staunch
ally for the LGBTQIA+ community and she will dress down
anyone who isn't.

If you're going to be an ally, you have to be ready to fight, not just when the situation suits you. You can't have riveting, well-written TV shows, stylish clothes, great pop music, basically the entire Broadway canon, and secretly vote to ban gay marriage and discrimination protections just because you're "fiscally conservative" and want the tax breaks. (I'd add that there's no such thing as socially liberal and fiscally conservative. That oxymoron has always struck me as denigrating.) Full marriage equality occurred on June 26, 2015, with the Supreme Court decision in Obergefell v. Hodges. But as we saw with Roe v. Wade, equal rights in this country are always precarious. Not that the institution of marriage is historically so great for straight women. For most of recorded history, women were the property of their fathers and then their husbands, no better than a pair of goats or a featherbed. Women couldn't even have their own credit cards without a man's signature until fifty years ago—so within Memaw Pumps's lifetime. The idea that this is in dispute is anathema to me.

When I was thirteen, my mother and I used to get our hair done by a man named Roland. Since it was the eighties, I went to the hairdresser every six weeks to get my hair permed. I wanted to look like Daryl Hannah in *Splash*, but the perm made me look like a poodle that stuck a fork in an electric socket. The eighties were very, very bad for fashion, especially in Oklahoma. Everything was bold stripes, side ponytails, and ginormous hair. The shoulder pads had shoulder pads.

One day, my mom and I were getting into her car to go to the hair salon, when she said, "Jennifer, I've got to share something with you, darlin'. Roland is now going by Renee, and you must call her 'she.'"

This was long before anyone openly talked about being transgender, what pronouns to use, or people's dead names. I remember looking at my mom and thinking, *Okay, Mom, whatever you say.* It had a real impact on me, the way my mother normalized this. It changed the way I felt about people's affirmed gender and how it can differ from their gender assigned at birth. At the time, we didn't have the language around these concepts, and my mom may have said it differently, but I remember her support for Renee's expression of her true self.

Growing up a staunch atheist in a sea of Fundamentalists, I understood a little bit about what it was like to feel othered. When my friends took me to church, the preachers all said, "Homosexuali-*TEE*," with an emphasis on the last syllable. Saliva would fly out of their mouths across the pulpit. It made me think no matter how much they claimed to "support diversity" in their literature, no matter how much they bandied around the word *tolerance*, it seemed to me that even the most accepting among them were still just a pubic hair from praying the gay away. Remember: my parents didn't belong to a congregation, not just because they weren't practicing Christians, but because my mother couldn't stand even a lick of hypocrisy or narrow-mindedness. But the general timbre of these megachurches was to discriminate against anyone who went against the grain, and it made me sick. A lot of my gay friends had been subjected to religious-affiliated conversion therapy programs. Others were told they would burn in hell for the "sin" of being who they were. Even when I was a girl, I knew this was wrong, that if there was an equalizing force in the universe, or a hell, the only people going there would be the ones who subjected kids to this kind of psychological torture.

Years later, when my son Dylan was about two, my mother called to tell me about a sociology course she was auditing at a nearby college. Her Texas accent seemed more pronounced than usual, which indicated she was riled about something. Apparently, she'd just learned that in the 1950s, married men who were gay would tie scarves around their necks to signal their availability for sex when they were cruising for other men in local parks.

"It got me thinking," she said. "My daddy would stand in the mirror for hours getting ready to go to the park. He would tie this scarf around his neck. And then he would go to Bachman Lake without me or my little sister Margaret." She paused. "I think my daddy could have been gay."

"Wow," I said, looking at Dylan in his highchair. "Wow," I repeated. "How do you feel about that?"

"I feel like a lot of things make sense, darlin'. I remember he had this male friend he was always with, and they would get in these real dramatic fights . . ." She trailed off, and before I could ask her to expand on my grandfather's possible boyfriend, she said, "Let's go to the nursing home so we can ask Mama Worth if she thinks Worthy was gay."

Maybe this sounds like the beginning of a Tennessee Williams play, but I didn't have to think about my mother's request for one second. I grabbed Dylan, strapped him into his car seat, and drove about half an hour south to pick up my mother to go to my grandmother's nursing home. Mama Worth was meaner than a rattlesnake, the kind of person who could outlive a sequoia. Historically, she'd never been nice to my mother, but my mother still visited her dutifully every day to do her nails and fix her hair.

When we got to the nursing home, Mama Worth was in her usual armchair in front of her TV, Fox News blaring at decibel level thirty-seven.

"Mama Worth," I yelled because she was hard of hearing.

"Yes, honey?"

"Do you think Worthy was gay?"

"What, honey?"

"DO YOU THINK WORTHY WAS GAY?"

She looked up from an ad for Lipitor. "Oh, he was absolutely as gay as a two-dollar bill," she said. "And his sister, Ella, was a big ol' lesbian. She never got married, and she dipped tobacco."

My mother's eyes flashed, and Mama Worth said nothing further on the subject. She just turned back to the TV, as though the commercial for Depends was the second coming, and the Messiah would rise to save us all, wearing nothing but a pair of adult diapers.

"I guess some people just feel like they can't come out of the closet and have to get married," my mother said to no one. I could tell she was wrestling with the notion, reassessing her ideas about her parents and their marriage. How could this woman, her mother, who had criticized everything she had done her whole life, be so accepting of her husband's sexuality? Was life in the closet emblematic of the Silent Generation, the idea of living one life publicly and another behind closed doors? Were we all doing this to a certain extent now with social media? Pretending our lives were happy and glamorous when they ran the gamut from mundane to challenging? I'd left so many things unsaid in my own marriage. Swept so much under the rug to have an easier afternoon without bickering, but was this dishonest living or just picking my battles?

When we got back in the car, my mother was quiet for a moment, pulling her seat belt across her lap. A storm was rolling in and the clouds sat low and gray over the wheat fields.

"Do you really think Ella was a lesbian?" my mother asked. I signaled as I turned onto the freeway.

"I don't know, Mom," I said. "Sure as hell sounds like it. Sounds like everyone was."

"Worthy and his male friend used to write each other very long letters. Worthy had the most elegant cursive."

"I don't know if good handwriting means anything in terms of someone's sexuality, Mom," I said.

"Maybe they were having an epistolary romance, Jennifer," she said. Her voice had a sharp tone, signaling the end of the discussion. I decided not to press her further.

Had Mama Worth been Worthy's beard all those years? Had they never loved each other, only held each other in high regard? Had Mama Worth experienced any real physical affection in her relationship with my grandfather? Had she ever felt any affection for anyone? I don't know. She certainly never doled much of it out. Every marriage is a black box, and nobody except that couple knows what happens inside it. I do know this: Mama Worth was an alcoholic and an unrepentant racist—in other words, a tough woman to love. Yet, she'd married a gay man who'd went on to live his entire life in the closet, sneaking off to have sex with other people, who were most likely all men. This didn't soften my opinion toward her, or her politics, as much as broaden my understanding of her loneliness, a feeling I'd often experienced in my own marriage.

Sometimes people list all of Josh's supposedly "gay" (metrosexual) attributes: great haircut, stylish designer clothes, statement eyewear, and generally artsy demeanor. I want to tell them I know so many gay men who have horrible hair and wear bad clothes—though maybe this is just Oklahoma. My husband loves nothing more than monochromatic dressing. However, I know from all of my gay friends that Grindr is chock-full of supposedly straight married men cruising for tail. I guess people have moved from tying scarves around their necks to scrolling the apps. I just wish my Grandfather Worthy could have lived out loud as a proud gay man. For some reason, even in 2024, it's easier to accept a bad straight marriage than a good gay one. It's more socially acceptable to be a straight man, marry multiple times, and grab women by the pussy than it is to bake a wedding cake for same-sex couples and stick two brides on the top tier. You'd think with all the TV shows and movies with LGBTQIA+ characters (including on Disney), we would have evolved our stance on this topic.

Case in point: Pumps. She grew up Evangelical and praying on it, and now the only thing she worships is Rachel Maddow. She grew up in a world where she was taught homosexuality was an abomination, and now she proudly wears a T-shirt that reads MOTHER in rainbow letters. She stands up to people who make homophobic or racist slurs. She votes Democrat. And if Memaw Pumps can do it, if she can evolve, someone who grew up indoctrinated, so can anyone. It starts with listening. Then questioning. Then standing up in the voting booth. I'm not a single-issue voter—I have a lot of issues, believe me—but I go hard in the paint for LGBTQIA+ rights. I will fight for gay kids with my last dying breath because for so many of them, their first bullies were their parents, pastors, and megachurches. My grandfather has been dead many years now, but I feel his spirit in my car when certain maudlin country songs come on my Spotify, and the empty road stretches out like a wide, dark ribbon in front of me, full of hope and possibility.

PAIN MANAGEMENT

~~~~~~~~~~

ANGIE

TWO WEEKS BEFORE I went to rehab, I was watching *Dopesick*, a TV show on Hulu about the opioid crisis starring Michael Keaton. I binged the whole series, high as a kite on morphine and Percocet, thinking, *At least, I'm not on OxyContin . . .*

Every month, I peed in a cup. A bevvy of medical professionals checked my pee to make sure my levels were proper. My pee was legal. Everything was legal.

Legal, legal, legal.

Bless these poor addicts' hearts, I thought, dry swallowing my sixth Perc.

The whole pill problem started in 2011 with a herniated disc. I was in so much pain I could hardly function. Even in July, I was driving with the heated seats on high. So, when my doctor suggested back surgery, I agreed. I trusted him to fix me. But a few months after the surgery, wouldn't you know, that darn disc reherniated. So, I tarzanned right back to the surgeon who went right in and "fixed that sucker" one more time. A year later the same disc herniated. Again. So, I fixed it. *Again.* But then, the pain came back much worse. I couldn't walk, stand, crawl, sit, or lie down for love or money.

I started to think the universe was punishing me for something I'd done in a past life. But Jennifer informed me the universe didn't work like that.

"The universe is just a vast series of cold, lonely galaxies, one after the other, repeating out into infinity," she said. Then she started mouthing off flat-earthers. I knew what she meant, but how would laughing about redneck conspiracy theories help me with my damn back pain? Couldn't she see I was at my breaking point?

After yet another MRI, the doctor called me—you know you're in a whole heap of trouble when the doctor calls you personally—and told me even though there was a less than 1 percent chance that the same disc would re-herniate, mine had. He offered me two options: One was to cut through my stomach and put two rods and twelve screws into my back, after which I'd be bedridden for three months, therefore not an option. I had a husband who was mostly MIA and we had three kids, none of whom drove, and all of whom had ninety-five different activities in ninety-seven different places, eight days a week. I was the short-order cook, the nanny, the housekeeper, the math tutor, the social secretary, the laundress, the baker, and the chauffeur.

The second option was to kick me into "pain management," which meant two twelve-hour morphine tablets and six Percocet per day. Obviously, I chose what was behind door number two. *That sounds totally manageable*, I thought. *I can handle taking morphine. Maybe everyone else is just weak.*

Soon, I stopped feeling those sharp edges. I stopped feeling much of anything. My husband may have been getting his jollies at the Bare Assets strip club, but I was way too doped up to care. Kirk would be busy "working" until nine o'clock, then he'd come home to sleep in the guest room while I watched my iPad until I passed out in the living room. That's how disparate our lives were. We divided and conquered the kids' nine million activities on the weekends, but we never spent more than two hours a week together, if that. At the end of the day, the effect of the Percocet and the morphine created a soft, cotton bunting between me and the rest of the world. My chronic pain seemed to go away. Kirk would ask me a question, or he'd lie to my face, and I'd feel next to nothing.

But the Percs were a cheap trick designed to keep my true feelings at bay. They made the intolerable seem tolerable. Later, I would learn that the reason opioids are so physically addictive is that they send a sensor to your brain that your body is in severe physical pain, tricking your mind into believing it's in constant need of the meds. Ultimately, I had to retrain the nerve receptors in my brain to feel anything at all, let alone what they expected. But what was expected? I had no effing clue.

Something like fifty-one million Americans suffer from chronic pain, some with no obvious physical cause, others from autoimmune disease, illness, or injuries they sustain at work or home. I had a herniated disc, as many people do.

But if you were to give fifty random people MRIs, some of those people would have herniated or bulging discs and feel *zero* pain. Why? A doctor from NYU named John Sarno suggested another possibility. Repressed emotions show up somewhere, and sometimes, they rear their ugly heads as debilitating physical pain. Yep. A herniated disc is a perfect exit route for emotional pain dying to get to the surface.

For me, the key to treating this disabling physical pain wasn't to pile on more pain management. Instead, I had to examine the actual *emotions* at the core of the pain—the ones I was trying so hard to avoid. Of course, even though I watch *Chicago Med*, and *ER*, I'm no medical doctor and can't diagnose anyone. Everyone should go to their medical doctor to check any persistent pain to make sure it isn't the sign of a larger problem. But why did I keep having pain in the same disc after three surgeries? Why did the doctor simultaneously prescribe me both drugs? Couldn't he see that I was higher than a Russian satellite? Was he ever going to say, "This bitch has been on these addictive pain pills for a decade. Time to cut her the fuck off." The bigger question: What darkness was I avoiding like a skunk at a garden party? Why did I feel too chickenshit to turn on the lights?

For so long, my default setting was denial. But no matter how many pills I swallowed or shows I binged on Netflix until my brain turned to cottage cheese, my nervous system still felt everything I was trying to ignore. It knew there was a lot of muck down there I didn't want to confront. Maybe it was time to consider the emotional causes of my back pain and come up with a strategy that didn't involve morphine, six Percocet, MSNBC, Dick Wolf, and my bathrobe.

The watershed moment came one spring break when Jennifer's family and my family all went to Mexico on vacation together, minus Kirk, who stayed back in OKC to "work." I thought it was a typical vacation. The kids swam and snorkeled. I got too much sun and took long naps on the beach. When we got back, I popped a Perc and washed it down with some Diet Coke. I was about to get in the shower when my phone vibrated.

I'm sick of this, Jen texted. **I should have said something a long time ago, but I thought you were fucked up in Mayakoba.**

And I thought, *Me? Fucked up? No fucking way. I am managing my chronic pain. Watch. Me. Manage.*

My oldest son, Sam, saw that text Jennifer sent in the cloud. He called her and told her he knew something was going on with me. Then he called my parents, who told my brother. My parents, Jennifer, my kids, and my brother staged an intervention, and I left the next day for rehab in Atlanta. It was a six-week program, but in the end, I stayed for eight weeks.

In rehab, I felt so much shame that I'd hurt my kids, but mostly I just *felt*. I felt everything. Every feeling, even ones from my early childhood. My biological father had left when I was three. His split from my mother had been amicable. I saw him growing up, but I thought of my stepdad as my father and my biological father as the fun guy who took me out to dinner and bought me beer when I was in high school. I'd always told myself that I was totally fine about my parents' divorce because it had happened when I was too young to know better, but rehab made me wonder if that was actually true. Memories surfaced of my bio dad and me at Lake Texoma, his big hand in mine as I asked him about alligators. At night, I dreamed of a shadowy figure walking out the door. Or a tall man in a cowboy hat walking around the corner, someone I tried to catch up with but couldn't.

Sometimes, I lay awake at night thinking of Kirk and his addiction to sex. The way I could smell cheap bodywash on his shirts when I took them out of the hamper. The more I thought about it, the angrier I got. I would hunch over the toilet bowl, dry heaving. When we got married, Kirk had promised me the moon and the stars. We had a house with a pool, three kids in private school, two nice cars. All the stuff America teaches us to want. He may have been leading a double life, but the pills were such a limp-dick move on my part. I abandoned my goals and dreams for a marriage that wasn't fulfilling. I became a stoned, soggy cardboard cutout of my prior self.

I went to rehab in the early, dark days of the pandemic, when we were still washing the groceries and preparing to die alone on ventilators. My Family Week happened like everything did back then, on Zoom, one soul-destroying session after another. First with Jennifer, then my kids, then my mother. Sam read from a letter he'd written detailing all the separate instances he'd seen me under the influence, which, because I had been high on pills for years, were a lot of instances. One night I'd nodded off on the porch watching *I'll*

Be Gone in the Dark on my iPad and didn't come to until the next day, when the kids woke up to go to school and found me passed out in my robe.

"Luke and Emily don't know you as a real mom," Sam read. "They don't know the difference between you being on pills and the mom I know. But I know the difference. I remember the difference."

I still think about what Sam said. How what I did will stain my kids' childhoods forever and I can never change that. I can never eliminate that blight. All I ever wanted was to be a mother. All I wanted was to provide my kids with a safe place to land, but I abandoned my post for a handful of Percs. After I got clean, I wandered my house at night, so sober I felt drunk again, trying to figure out how to right the wrong of blanketing my pain with opioids like I was an extra on *Dopesick.*

When I called my sponsor, she reminded me of a concept from The Big Book, aka the bible of AA, called a "living amends," which is the part of your recovery where you commit to modifying your present and future choices. Instead of making direct amends for something you did in the past—the Ninth Step—a living amends pays it forward by living the promise of thoughtful behavior *going forward.* Since you can't change the past, sometimes a living amends means doing the right thing *right now* rather than dwelling forever on what you did wrong *then.* The trick is to do the next right thing one day at a time.

Which brings me back to my back pain. The doctor would ask me to rate it on a scale of one to ten, with ten being the

worst, and I would say, "FIFTY." Maybe the pain was covering my rage. Ever since my bio dad walked out when I was
three, I sought out men who had one foot out the door. That
was my part in it: I set up another situation with a phantom
presence and built a house of rage around it. The question
was, what was I going to do about it now?

Sometimes it feels like painful feelings are here to stay but
guess what? They always pass. I know now, when I'm sitting
with intense anger, anxiety, sadness, grief, fear—or any mix
of negative emotions—that I'm strong enough to endure
intense discomfort without reaching for a pill bottle. Instead,
when I start to feel myself spiral, I take ten deep breaths.
Then I call my sponsor. Or one of my sisters from Kappa
Kappa Gamma. Or Jennifer. Someone to remind me of how
far I've come and how strong I am. As much as I wanted an
illustrated how-to manual, I needed someone to remind me
of who I was. I had to train my mind until I broke that sucker
in like a wild stallion on *Yellowstone*.

I'd grown up thinking a lot about Jesus. My life revolved
around His deeds and worship. My instruction manual was
the Bible. Now, when I'm at a Third Step meeting, which
is a meeting where you're supposed to let go and let God, I
don't think about the Father, the Son, or the Holy Ghost.
I think about the holy trinity of my three kids. I recall the
brutally honest text from Jennifer that got me sober in the
first place. The truth hurts. Pain *hurts*. And then, slowly, so
slowly, it doesn't.

HAVING KIDS WON'T SOLVE YOUR PROBLEMS

JEN

BELIEVE IT OR NOT, I played with baby dolls when I was a child. You'd think I would have pretended to be Barbara Walters, or Oprah, interviewing my stuffed animals until they wept silent tears after I broke them down, getting them to reveal their deepest secrets. Nope. I pretended to be a mother. In the eighties, the "it" toy was the Cabbage Patch doll; I had two of them. A Black one and a white one. They came with adoption papers and separate outfits you could buy. All the girls I knew had them. We would all get together with our Cabbage Patch dolls for playdates. Looking back on it now, it's so clear that society, assisted by the brute force of capitalism, was brainwashing us to want to be moms. All the commercials on TV at the time were gender specific. (Let's face it, most still are.) The little girls would be combing My Little Pony's purple hair or playing with Baby Alive, whose diaper they joyously changed when she peed and pooped, while the boys raced cars or built blocks or saved the universe from the Dark Side with their Lightsabers.

None of this early childhood play helped me in the least. No doll baby or Safe Sitter class can prepare anyone for the hard-hitting, twenty-four-hour-a-day physical and emotional reality of being a parent. When Josh and I had Dylan, we had only been dating for about a year. We were not remotely prepared for what it meant to suddenly have this crying whelp dependent on us for comfort and sustenance. I clung to the adages: I was born to do this. Families fix everything. Motherhood is the goal.

Those tired old saws didn't help either.

Prior to my getting pregnant, Josh and I would meet up with our friends and hit the town to party. After I found out I was knocked up, I assumed Josh would want to stay home and nest. I thought we would prepare healthy dinners together and snuggle on the sofa, watching TV as our baby grew in my belly. Instead, Josh amped his partying into overdrive. I would later discover that people who suffer from severe childhood trauma, like Josh had, subconsciously muddle over their own childhood when their partner is pregnant, exacerbating negative coping mechanisms. When I look back on it now, I think, *Jesus H. Christ, why were we breeding?* But the answer is we fell deeply in love.

While Josh was out coping, I was at home, clinging to the idea that once our baby was born, all would improve in the cabbage patch. I felt a level of loneliness and depression that I'd never experienced before. Remembering my pregnancy, even now, is a source of gut-wrenching pain. My dad had his own issues, but for all his shortcomings, he was very loyal to our family unit. His presence might not have always been pleasant, but there he was, sober as a judge at the dinner table, or out in the pigeon loft tending to his birds. If he wasn't home, he was driving somewhere to race them. So, my default setting was to stick with Josh no matter what. Josh, on the other hand, was raised like a wild dog. His own father started drinking with him when Josh was a young boy. When his dad wasn't sucking down the hooch at home, he was out on the town, leaving Josh to fend for himself.

Until Josh went to rehab in 2002, he'd spent his whole life drunk. His mother tried to take her own life when Josh was five years old, and Josh was the one who found her near lifeless body, her pulse thin and reedy. Then, his dad shipped Josh's mother off to a psychiatric hospital in Tulsa, with zero explanation about where she had gone. All Josh knew was that his discovery of his mother led to her sudden unexplained absence. She died of cancer when he was in law school. On her deathbed, she apologized to Josh for leaving him so many times and he forgave her. But I often wondered, how much water do these deathbed apologies hold? If you dug down beneath the mantle, would you find five-year-old Josh repeatedly stumbling onto his mother's body? It wasn't lost on me that he would later end up leaving our kids multiple times too. Not deliberately, but when he went into treatment. Was history repeating itself?

There's a level of cognitive dissonance necessary to sustain any marriage on the best of days. Sometimes it's hard enough to listen to your spouse tell a long story about their workday or describe a dream they had or to listen to them chew. There were times when I hated the way Josh breathed. You could hardly call either of us wallflowers, so when we argued, it was like two rams running at each other. Nobody backed down. But after the ramming subsided, there was a strong desire to let cooler heads prevail.

When Angie was going through her stuff with Kirk, she kept saying, "I wish Kirk would just die. Then my problems would be solved." Maybe it would have been simpler to feel that way about Josh, but I didn't. I couldn't conjure a black-and-white view of our relationship. I could still see the real Josh under his dysfunction. The intelligent, wild thinker driving me around Oklahoma when we were courting. The person whose emotions were right there on the surface. I still felt so much love for him. When Josh relapsed, I never wanted to fan the flame of my kids' resentments or their justifiable feelings of disappointment about their father. I defended him—the real him, the sober him—even as I swooped in multiple times and said, "As much as you feel disappointed in him right now, at the other side of this addiction, a sober, loving version of your dad is more mortified than you are."

I would lay down my life for my family but being a mom to young kids isolated me from the rest of the world. I was so focused on their needs and the repetitive tasks required to fulfill those needs that I had little time to focus outward and connect with others. Being in any constant caretaker role is often thankless, whether it's being a mother to small children or an adult caring for elder, infirm parents. Or if you're a sibling or close friend to someone with health issues. My whole life was work and the demands of my family unit. This was another thing that bonded Angie and me. We could be with our kids and speak honestly with each other.

I remember going to wake Dylan up from his nap one afternoon. He'd taken off his diaper and smeared poop all over the rails of his crib and the wall. It took the longest time to get the poop out from under my fingernails and the smell out of the walls. Of course, when I was done, I called Pumps and told her about Diapergate.

"Emily did that once," she said, referring to her daughter, who was about the same age.

It made me feel better to know that Pumps was also out there in Nichols Hills, scrubbing shit off her own walls. It made me feel less crazy about the fevers and the long nights alone with human excrement under my fingernails while my husband was out partying with adults who pooped into actual toilets. While those early years were emotional trench warfare, I have zero regrets about having my boys. Zero. My kids transformed my life and brought me back to myself. Dylan's dexterity with language and his innate wisdom, Roman's grounded presence, and athleticism—the way he can sum any moment in one perfect phrase. His quiet sense of humor. Watching them grow into their authentic selves has been the greatest joy of my life.

But Josh's rejection of our home when I was pregnant and during the first few years of my children's lives traumatized me. The memory of pacing the halls of our old house, holding Dylan, holding Roman, shushing them while they cried. I lived in terror of opening the door to a state trooper telling me Josh had died in a drunk-driving accident—or worse, getting a call that he had killed someone while drunk driving. Sometimes, cleaning the kitchen for the five-hundredth time, I wished that I was the addict so I wouldn't have to solo parent.

I see so much unrealistic content on social media about parenthood and family. When I see these posts, I don't think, *Look at Paisleigh. She is crushing motherhood. Her husband, Kashton, is such a supportive stud! Look at that stunning fall tablescape!* I think about all the broken young men and women struggling to make it through the day. Struggling to put food on the table. I think about how hard adulthood and parenthood actually are, the grit and the grace of it. Having kids only exacerbates your existing problems, it doesn't erase them. Kids make you more of who you are, not less. Unless you tend to it, generational family dysfunction seeps through the cracks no matter what you do.

Sometimes, my mind wanders to those Cabbage Patch dolls, and I think about all the malarkey I was sold about being a parent. Although Josh and I somehow rose to the occasion, it was a long shot. I wish I had gotten my act together sooner. (Does anyone have their act together?) I wish someone had indoctrinated me with the reality that the walls would be smeared with shit, but there would be pizza and belly laughs. Having little kids might be bad for overall quality of life, but in the end, Josh and I created these two perfect humans who are better people than we could ever hope to be. They didn't solve our problems. But they've made our lives more fulfilling.

SUNDAY SCHOOL DROPOUT

~~~~~~

ANGIE

WHEN I WAS A young mom, I taught Bible study to a bunch of other Evangelical women at my church. What my qualifications were for this job, I don't rightly know, except my mother had done it and she thought I should do it. I'd never formally studied the Bible or theology, and I had zero training beyond attending Sunday school and taking a similar Bible study course taught by a similarly unschooled teacher for two years. At the time, I believed the Bible was the word of God, and not only that, Christ Jesus was my only salvation. I believed in miracles, not the Catholic kind, like Mary's face on the side of a barn, but I believed in virgin birth. I wouldn't have been too surprised if someone spoke in tongues. I believed whole hog in the pageantry of the church. And I believed Jesus died for my sins, but what were those sins exactly? Gossiping? Eating too many Mrs. Fields cookies at the mall? Chugging too much Orange Julius?

Back then, everyone I knew went to church. We're talking Oklahoma. Not only was everyone I knew Christian, but everyone was Evangelical, which meant participating blindly in a codependent relationship with Jesus. The program was called BSF, an acronym for Bible Study Fellowship, and it met once a week from 9 to 11 a.m. I taught Moses, Noah, Acts of the Apostles, all the greatest hits. The format was pretty standard: We'd read a few pages of biblical text and then tootle off into our little breakout groups to answer questions from a workbook, then reconvene for a riveting lecture on the excerpt. When I look back on that time, I don't recognize myself. Or maybe I do, but that woman seems abstract and far away. The other gals in the class were all nice, young moms like me, raising kids around the same age as mine. There was a lot of swapping of practical information about things like Diaper Genies and sleep training. We all commiserated about how much work it was to exist as a mother.

Sometimes I wonder, as an ex-Evangelical, how did I believe everything I said I believed? Devout religion is funny like that; in some way, it's the apex of habit, belief, and tradition. It's hard to delineate fact from fiction, belief from blind faith and desire. Did I seriously think a burning bush talked to Moses? Maybe not. But then again, I also accepted everything at face value. I thought Sarah and Abraham had a baby at ninety. The day I realized that Jesus didn't write the New Testament, that other people reported His word, I thought, *Is everything just a massive game of telephone?*

I remember taking the kids to the dinosaur exhibit at the Museum of Natural History, an unremarkable outing for most parents. The whole scene was controlled chaos with screaming children everywhere. I don't like museums, my feet hurt, and I get bored and thirsty after about five minutes. But I sat staring at a Tyrannosaurus rex, thinking, *How does this work? How did the dinosaurs walk the earth two thousand years ago? How did they fit on the Ark?* Even though I was teaching Bible study, there was always a part of me that questioned the cosmic data. This is the funny thing about religion, I believed a bush talked, but I also believed in science and medicine. And that was my quandary. I started examining everything from all sides. Including the cold, hard fact that there was no way that humans and dinosaurs coexisted on God's earth (or anybody's earth for that matter). Forget that my Sunday school teachers had taught me otherwise; I'd upheld this distorted version of reality much longer than I care to admit, as in, into adulthood.

But I didn't voice any of these concerns. When you're in a tight-knit, religious community, you don't just raise your hand on a Sunday morning and say, "Hey, Evelyn, did that Red Sea actually part so that the Israelites could escape the Egyptians? Did that *really* happen, or is it a big metaphor for surviving an impossible situation? Please pass the Snickerdoodles." What, if anything, did my students and peers believe? I never asked any of those women, just like I never questioned anything. Just like I never thought anybody else in the whole, wide world could ever have problems as fucked up as mine. I never looked behind the door. I never went into the basement.

I remember sitting in some breakout group while a very nice woman answered a question about Passover, thinking, *I wish someone had smeared blood on my door and my house got passed over.* But then I thought, *You're not supposed to think that.* Even as I thought, *This stuff doesn't aid or comfort me anymore. My problems extend beyond the parameters of this book. There are no answers for me here.* It was a huge crisis of faith. The beginning of the end. Everything that I'd been taught my whole life no longer applied to what was happening in my actual life. I couldn't pray it away.

Keep in mind, I knew Kirk wasn't like other husbands. (See under: rug burns.) But I kept trying my darnedest to stuff that brutal reality under the proverbial rug. First of all, I'd been told my whole life I was the golden child and I irrationally believed this descriptor would offer me some sort of protection. I'd also assumed a direct line to God would preclude anything terrible from happening. Then, of course, it turned out no one has a direct line to God, least of all me. Many other, more intelligent people have written about whether or not God exists, so I won't bore you with that (see under: Nietzsche), but instead of questioning myself or my broken picker, I went down the rabbit hole of questioning my natal faith. (Mom, if you're reading this, skip to the next page or possibly the next chapter.) I questioned God and Jesus and the Bible they rode in on. I prayed to be a better pray-er if that makes any sense. But it didn't work. The more I thought, *I can fix it. Fix him. Fix us*, the more broken and disconnected I felt.

Nothing worked. All the prayers felt like cheesy love songs from the seventies, the spiritual equivalent of singing "The Piña Colada Song" and expecting some kind of epiphany.

Then my biological father died of complications from diabetes, and it caused a fracture between my thinking mind and spiritual mind. I started interrogating everything. I started deconstructing my faith, meaning I turned to other scientific and philosophical sources for answers. I examined the supposedly infallible suppositions of my faith under a microscope. It's hard to describe everything my dad meant to me because he hadn't been a daily presence in my life the way my stepdad had. I didn't see him that often. He left when I was three. He was more of the "fun party dad" to my stepdad's "reliable, good Christian dad," but he was a big thinker. He painted a bigger picture of the wider world, one that stuck with me. His ideas and opinions lingered in the periphery of my thinking when I was at church. I noticed a bunch of things I'd turned a blind eye to before, like extreme nationalism and antigay sentiment, which suddenly stood out in bold relief. These oppressive ideologies no longer sat right with me. I started to feel sick about it all. About myself. I couldn't sleep. Sometimes, I could barely eat a bowl of cereal. Other times, I'd be in my kitchen, eating shredded cheese straight out of the bag at 4 a.m.

As time passed, I stopped going to church and attending or teaching Bible study. I never talked to my parents about it. I didn't tell anybody but Jennifer. But I just couldn't stomach the antigay, pro-Christ agenda for another second. Yes, on some level, I wanted Sunday mornings to myself. So, on the surface, you could say I quit the Son of God for a few extra hours of sleep. Having three kids is an awful lot of driving, and Kirk was always "working late at his office." The onus often fell on me to be the number-one schlepper. But my departure from the church was about so much more than that. My whole life started to feel out of sync and fake, like it would if you turned to me and said, "Now live according to *Game of Thrones.*" I didn't know how to do it anymore. I didn't know how to do anything.

I haven't been to church in over a decade, except when my mom asks me to go with her for Easter or Mother's Day. Even though I rise when I'm supposed to and mouth the familiar words when I'm supposed to, I feel as disconnected as my kids doing Zoom school during the pandemic.

I'm not saying religion is bad. Or that Jesus isn't nice. He had great abs and I'm sure he was a great guy. I think everyone should do what's right for them. Today, there are plenty of LGBTQIA+ affirming religious organizations. But it seems to me that bigotry still runs rampant, even among megachurches that call themselves "liberal." When Jennifer and I are on the signing line after our live podcasts, so many of our fans tell us about how their megachurch-attending families disowned them when they came out or how they forced them to participate in conversion therapy. It always upsets me to my core, not just the pain people had to endure, but the way religious groups exclude a whole swath of humanity in the name of a holy book they for sure aren't living.

So, when other Evangelical moms I know claim to adhere entirely to the Word, when they use phrases like "I am walking in freedom from sin," I just smile and wave like a beauty contestant because I've learned the hard way that it's not worth it to get into an argument about the Big Man Upstairs with a Bible thumper. They claim to be saved but I know that isn't true because I thought I was saved, and I was anything but. That's why I seek out the people who are brave enough to admit their lives are a total shitstorm. The people who fled with only the clothes on their backs. The people who don't pretend to have all the answers. These folks possess the kind of clarity our world needs.

One morning, before I got sober, I went down to the kitchen only to find it doused in oil and flour. I wiped a finger through a sticky puddle of syrup on the countertop. A used pan lay on the range, some brown substance burned into the bottom. I yelled upstairs for my kids. I couldn't believe they'd made such a mess. After a few minutes, Sam wandered into the kitchen.

"What the hell happened here?" I said.

"Um, Mom, you had a French toast party last night," he said.

"Oh," I said, vaguely recalling how I'd popped extra Percs the night before and entered some sort of culinary fugue state. "Right."

Who was I to judge anyone? I thought I had them all fooled. After all that Bible study and teaching, you'd think I would have learned a thing or two about the Ultimate Authority. You think I would have garnered more redemptive wisdom about how to live. But rescue is a myth. In the end, I had to save myself.

ITALIA, AMORE MIO

~~~

JEN

HERE'S SOMETHING WHOLLY UNORIGINAL about me: I love Italy. It's not just that I love the art and the architecture, the food and the clothes, or the gelato. I love the history. Looking out over the Colosseum in Rome, I can feel a powerful force ionizing the air, as if the essence of the gladiators and ancient spectators were still in the stone. Before you get riled up thinking I see dead people or that I am about to open a New Age bookstore—I'm not. There are certain places in life where portals exist. Where you can feel something larger than yourself.

In front of the Colosseum, I think about all it has seen, felt, and witnessed. Not just the history—the emperor who built the Colosseum, those who died brutal deaths within its walls, but how much time has elapsed and how much time will continue to elapse. Will another woman one day stand in front of this same structure two thousand years from now thinking the same thing with her family? Will it still be standing? Will humanity still exist, or will global warming kill us all?

If you've ever been to Pompeii, there's a famous plaster cast of a dying guard dog. The cast depicts the twisted body of a dog attempting to flee the heat and falling ash from Mount Vesuvius. Only the dog couldn't escape because its owners, who had likely fled to save their own lives, or were already dead, had left their dog to die, chained to its post. Whenever I saw these pictures in guidebooks, I was always more moved by this cast of the dog than by the casts of the bodies, who felt unknowable to me. Maybe because I always trusted dogs more than humans. It made me think of Tubby and Cha Cha. Or maybe because of the way the dog had died writhing but chained, attempting to escape the ash as it buried him. It felt personal, like I was the plaster cast of the twisted-up dog on a chain, left to suffocate under the molten ash.

My son Roman likes history and wants to major in political science when he goes to college. Dylan is a journalism major. Both view the world through the lens of a narrative that continually fractures and repeats like a kaleidoscope. Their viewpoint has informed mine. Ever since Roman read *Lord of the Flies* in ninth grade, he's been fascinated by the way the human mind naturally leans toward creating power structures. Maybe this is what those people were doing in those caves in Lascaux twenty-two thousand years ago. Making burnt offerings and creating societies.

I used to think my little problems were so huge. Every unaccounted pill of Josh's seemed bigger than an Airbus. Every fifteen-minute exchange with my husband could become a two-hour unpacking and analysis session with Pumps or Dr. K. or whomever else would listen. But when I'm in Italy, my mind views the universe in a different, more expansive way. Touring the Roman Forum, looking at the ruins and the pot shards, all my grievances seem so petty and small. A dot on a timeline. Every step along those ancient cobbles reminds me that, in the grand scheme of things, our problems and even our lives are just a blip.

I'm not saying my problems don't count, quite the opposite. Life is a shitstorm of fuckery that can bring you to your knees, some real dark-night-of-the-soul-type fuckery. In my case, the fuckery taught me something. It taught me I was stronger than I thought. It taught me no one escapes the fuckery; in fact, there is a continuum of fuckery that stretches all the way back to the time of the Colosseum and even before that. Greece, Sumer, Babylon. Fuckery for days.

Recently, I was on a boat bound from Naples for Capri, my absolute favorite place on earth, a place where the air smells like lemon zest, the tennis courts are clay, the navy sea laps against the cliffs, and I feel fully alive, fully myself. My personal live, laugh, love. As the boat sped across the water, all I could think about (aside from sipping an espresso in La Piazzetta) was the Blue Grotto, a sea cave where the sunlight shines through an underwater cavity, giving the water a magical glow. It was a place that defied description, a place I crave when I'm back in the States, walking the produce aisle at Target. But when I'm at the Grotto, the beauty of it almost overwhelms me. I find myself growing maudlin, trying to capture every ripple of the water, every crag of the rock. I remembered being on a boat with my son, Dylan, and his girlfriend, enjoying myself but silently weeping over the bow. Was I trying to make meaning out of some essentially meaningless family vacation? Some little blip in the arc of time?

But that's exactly what life is—finding a place you love and staying there. You stay. You commit. You weather the ash. You live with the broken statuary that is your marriage, the fights and the sex and the creamy, delicious gelato that you ate together once laughing on a cobbled street, that yummy *gelateria* that you could never find again, though you tried and tried, walking in circles in sandals that were cute but gave you horrible blisters. You live with the disappointment painted in frescos across the walls. You live with love and all its pieces— and you hope you have enough Super Glue to put everything back together in time.

SINGLE PRINGLE

~~~~~~~~

ANGIE

BACK WHEN I WAS still married, if I wanted to go out of town with my friends, Kirk was all for it, because then I was off his radar. This meant I could prioritize my friendships, women whose company I preferred over my then-husband's. I could go on girls' trips and have girls' nights out and sip-and-sees; that was important to me. I felt like he was so open-minded, but really, he just never wanted me in his business.

People say the most stressful life events are moving, death of a loved one, job loss, illness, and divorce. All of these events are heinous, especially moving. I would almost rather lose a toe or an eye or possibly a hand than ever move again. The idea of looking at all that formal dinnerware that I have never used, and thinking about whether I should keep or toss it makes me want to flush my head down the toilet. A soup tureen. Really? Who did I think I was? And while I would never want to go through another divorce (my divorce proceedings were like scrubbing a sunburn with a Brillo pad and then rubbing the wound with lemon and Tabasco sauce), my life *after* the divorce was heaven on 1.5 acres.

I recently bought airplane tickets for all three of my kids to see the live podcast of *I've Had It* in San Francisco. The fact that I could afford to buy those tickets with my own money was such a kick. Even more wonderful was that my kids loved the show and were proud of me, their hot mess of a mom who used to be passed out in a bathrobe on the front porch! But I'm getting ahead of myself.

Going back to work as a lawyer after thirteen years was more challenging than I thought it would be. The world had stopped using fax machines, apparently. If you say, "Xerox," to a Gen Z person, they might say, "What's that?" Also, I now had to earn money and come home and solo parent my three children whose sole provision and care was now a hundred percent my responsibility. Each kid had a different activity every day of the week. Everyone needed money for school trips, cheer costumes, dance costumes, and soccer cleats. Every night, I would pull into the garage and practice deep breathing because when I walked through the door, three people would be looking for me to feed them, help them with homework, take them somewhere, find their clothes, wash their clothes, and otherwise be their loyal servant.

But at the same time, I was a different kind of free. I was single for the first time in forever. I saw money coming into my bank account that I'd earned my own damn self. I wasn't snooping in anyone's phone. My heart felt like a frozen lump of clay, but it mysteriously continued to beat. Except for my yearly trip to the ob-gyn for a pap smear, I'd almost forgotten

I had a vagina. Sometimes I'd be peeing, and I'd look down between my legs and think, *Oh hi. I remember you. You birthed my babies, but you also got me into a ton of trouble.*

Back when I was still married, when Kirk went to rehab for sex addiction, I was so numb that a train could have run me over, and I wouldn't have noticed. It's hard to say what I was most upset about: Kirk's inability to control his ding-dong, or the fact that my marriage was over. I'd stopped having sex with Kirk long ago. Just the idea of touching a hair on his arm made me want to hurl. We never even went on "date night." In fact, we barely communicated, except for when we had to get the kids from point A to point B.

After I threw Kirk out of the house, Jennifer and I started going to a popular gym in our neighborhood. One morning, I happened to bump into my ex-boyfriend from college. In case you were wondering, I did not look good. Jennifer has always kept herself fit and healthy but I was emaciated. My hair was falling out. I hadn't worn makeup in over a year. Keep in mind, this was still Oklahoma City, where most women wear full-glamour makeup to the grocery store. Also, my mother had taught me never to leave the house without my face on, even in an emergency. But the whole situation with Kirk had knocked the wind out of my sails.

While I looked like death, my ex-boyfriend looked damn good, not as good as he did in college but way better than certain soon-to-be-ex-husbands who shall remain nameless (KIRK). My ex was bald but hot. Even through the haze of my depression, I could see this. I don't mean grows-on-you hot. I mean, I-could-see-his-six-pack-through-his-T-shirt hot. We still had that easy rapport we used to have at ATO parties. He looked at my face while he talked to me, which my soon-to-be-ex-husband almost never did. I'd forgotten what it was like to have a man look me in the eye, to ask me questions about my life, and listen to the answers. He then asked me more questions. It was revolutionary.

My first workout session, predictably, was an unmitigated disaster. Still, I went back. I started selecting slightly cuter workout outfits. My ex-boyfriend-from-college and I started joking around and chatting by the leg press machine, where he gave me exercise tips or talked about the importance of protein in muscle building. Jennifer remarked occasionally that I was being flirty. One day, my ex told me my hair was pretty. To be perfectly honest, he might have even said, "Your hair looks nice." Or even, "You have hair." It didn't matter. It struck me that no one with XY chromosomes besides my dad had noticed my hair or told me I looked nice in fifteen years. Our chats gave me vertigo, like the gym was a rocking ship. It made me do crunches until the back of my neck ached and my belly grew taut as a drum. I'd like to say his attention to my workout circuits and our related machinations about them turned me on, but it had been a while since anything had turned me on, so those fluttery feelings in my stomach and elsewhere could have been arousal or nerves, but either way, it felt good to know I was alive. I didn't even find it boring when he painstakingly described his high-protein, low-glycemic diet.

The day before Kirk was due to come home from rehab,

I called my ex-boyfriend and said, "Hey. Can I come over to talk to you sometime today?" I could hear the whir of a blender in the background. I wasn't sure if he knew what I meant or even if I knew. I hadn't followed that plotline all the way to the end. Was I going to go over to my ex-boyfriend's house and rekindle our college romance? Or was I just going to have seggs for the first time in who knows how long?

"Sure," he said. I hung up, every nerve in my body on high alert.

I applied full makeup, like I was Tammy Faye Bakker going to a televised revival meeting. I put on earrings and a cute outfit. I teased my hair. Then I went into the backyard to call Jennifer.

"I need you to get over here right now," I said. "It's a 911 emergency. Meet me in the backyard."

While Jen loaded up the kids, which was no easy feat because they were still pretty little, I sat on my back porch, smoking. When she walked back there and got a load of me, all dolled up, she said, "What's going on here, Pumps?"

I took a drag of my cigarette. "I'm going to go fuck my ex-boyfriend. I'll be back in an hour."

"Get it!" she said, giving me a high five.

Thus began my first, last, and only affair which continued for a couple months and gave me two UTIs and a latex allergy but was totally worth every single second. I would go to my ex-boyfriend's apartment and fuck my brains out while the kids were at school. Somehow, I mostly continued to work out the entire time, though sometimes Jennifer would show up at the gym and I wouldn't be there because I was otherwise engaged. Did I fall in love? Not even close. Was the sex earth-shattering? It wasn't about that. Did we walk off into the sunset together holding hands? Not my thing. I still had tremendous affection for the guy. Being with him was like getting into a time machine and going back to my college days when I felt wild and free and happy. Maybe if I'd looked into his eyes while orgasming, I could've caught actual human feelings, but we both wisely avoided that. I hadn't had good sex—okay, *any* sex—since the early days with Kirk. The idea of developing an emotional attachment for a man was about as appealing as sodomizing myself with a cactus.

When all of Kirk's sex addiction issues came to the fore, I never thought, *Oh, this is because I'm unattractive or don't blow him enough*. I never had to sit down with our mediocre excuse for a therapist and say, "Why am I not woman enough? Am I yucky?" That wasn't my concern. The main thought I had was why hadn't the life I offered Kirk been enough? Why wasn't our family sacred enough for him to want to keep it intact? The more Kirk lied to me about his dalliances, the smaller I shrank, until I no longer recognized myself. That two-month affair with someone who was honest and actually cared about me and my wellbeing was a way to take my power back. Also, let's face it: sometimes you just have to get laid.

The last time I ever went over to my ex-boyfriend's house was on a Wednesday. After we did it for the last time, he made me a protein smoothie. Unlike Kirk, I couldn't have sex without emotion, and I started to feel icky. I was the sole responsible adult in my kids' lives. It was important for me to not get caught up in any external bullshit. I didn't want this nostalgic wave to develop into operatic swells of feeling. I wanted my kids to see me move on, to know it was possible. I wanted them to know they could count on me no matter what. So, I told him we couldn't see each other anymore and I went online and bought a bright purple vibrator.

My ex-boyfriend had taught me so much—to flex my foot when I was extending my leg on the leg press and to exhale while doing crunches. He also taught me that I could still have a quickie when the urge struck. He reminded me that I still had urges. That I was human. More hottie MILF than pathetic, codependent caretaker. He taught me to like myself again. Maybe, in some way, he needed to have an affair too. To remind himself that connection exists, like a ribbon across time, even when you can't feel it. And I needed to remember my rock-solid core.

EMBRACE TIME

~~~~~~~~

JEN

A COUPLE WEEKS BEFORE I was due to be induced with Dylan, my first child, I went to Target to grab some groceries. As I waddled up and down the aisles, tossing various items into my cart, all I could think about was the possibility of going into labor right then and there on one of those pool floaties shaped like a doughnut. My pregnancy seemed like it would never end. I remember hearing other women talking about how pregnancy was such a *magical time*, and I would think about how my experience didn't align with theirs at all. I wanted my baby to come out of my body. I wanted Josh to be sober. I wanted so many things I couldn't have.

Suddenly, I found myself in front of the dairy case, selecting a carton of Horizon Organic milk. As I reached my hand to the back of the fridge, I pulled out the farthest carton and checked the expiration date. It read December 29. I stood there, lost in thought, marveling. I was going to be induced on December 16. I think I even said, "I will have my baby before this milk expires."

I cannot tell you how comforting that moment was for me. My relationship was precarious. I didn't know what life would be like once we added a baby to the mix, but that milk's expiration date was real. It was a number in space and time. It reminded me that everything has an expiration date. Even if something terrible happens, my intense feelings surrounding it will become more manageable and less intense. I've learned that I can handle pretty much anything if I can mentally craft a timeline and remember that everything has a shelf life. This quiet moment in the dairy aisle at Target became one of my greatest coping skills.

Everything has an expiration date. Everything on Earth expires. Pain especially. Even acute pain over the end of a major romantic relationship or anger after the worst fight you can imagine. Sometimes grief is so big it fundamentally changes you. In that case, it's not necessarily about *healing*, it's about putting one foot in front of the other. I wanted my discomfort to be over so badly. My belly was so big I couldn't even see my feet on the linoleum, and I had to lean on the buggy. Now, I can't even access that discomfort. I remember feeling it, but I can't physically tap into the actual pain.

I like knowing that everything is ephemeral. It reminds me to be present in happy moments. When I'm out walking my dogs, I think about the trees and how long they've been on earth. I see the squirrels, jumping from branch to branch, and think about how they are carrying on the simple work of storing food like their ancestors before them. I have active moments of meditation while observing the beauty and ruthlessness of our planet. I think about what I can do to make sure my nest is better than the one I came from. I supposed that's the closest I will ever get to any type of communication with a larger force in the universe.

How can I leave my sons in a better place, knowing my time here is limited? I don't know how to fix the huge problems of the greater world, global warming, racism, or wars—I leave that to people much smarter than I am—but I do know how to help make sure my humans are good people who will go out into the world and do good things and stand up for what they believe in. I hope they marry good people—if they want to get married. I hope they're happy and pursue their passions. I hope this for all of Gen Z, that they be free from all this meaningless attachment to what was or worry about what will be.

When I was young, I felt immortal. Death existed, but only as an abstract concept that happened to old people, like Worthy, my mother's father. I tanned without sunscreen, smoked countless cigarettes, and mainlined candy. I didn't have the same sense of time passing that I do now. The way it sadistically and secretly runs out, like air leaking from an air mattress while you sleep. Kids make you notice its passage more acutely. How they go from babies to toddlers to teens so quickly. Wasn't I just a teenager myself, about to lose my virginity?

I remember thinking that event was the most important, earth-shattering thing ever to happen to a single human person. My mother had already had the sex conversation with me about contraception and how to avoid STDs and not get pregnant, a conversation that naturally made me want to crawl into a hole and die. Meanwhile, my boyfriend was Evangelical and had a lot of shame around lust. His parents had never uttered the word *sex*, probably not even to each other, let alone to him. But I talked with my mother about everything. If I had a question or wanted more details about some obscure historical fact, she'd grab an *Encyclopedia Britannica*—this was before the internet—and say, "Darlin', let's read about that." She had an expansive way of looking at the world, even if it was showing me an anatomical drawing of a penis.

Sometimes, if I'm complaining about the standard mortifications of aging, my mother says, "Don't forget that however old you are now, you're as young as you'll ever be. Twenty years from now you'll look back and envy this version of yourself." It makes me think fondly of that day in Target, how if I could, I'd go back just so I could hold my baby boy in my arms again. Whenever I feel bad about myself or where this world is headed, whenever I worry about how we are destroying the planet or wonder about Dylan and Roman's children's children's rights, when I panic about the future, I call my mother. She has a way of reframing things for me. Maybe it's her dry, Texas delivery that lends a folksy wisdom to whatever she says, or maybe it's her innate intelligence, but she can zero in on any situation and sum it up in a concise phrase that feels brand-new and like something you've heard a hundred times, a truism you're looking at with fresh eyes.

"Look down at your feet, darlin'," she says. "There you are."

THERE IN SPIRIT

~~~~~~~~

ANGIE

RECENTLY, I READ SOMETHING interesting Fred Rogers said about love, which I'll summarize here: Love isn't perfect. It's an active verb that contains a sense of struggle. To love someone—a friend, a spouse, or a family member—is to accept them for who they are *right now*, not who they were or who you hope they might one day become.

You probably know Fred Rogers as Mr. Rogers from *Mister Rogers' Neighborhood*, a show I watched when I was little, along with *Sesame Street* and *The Electric Company*. I just loved Mr. Rogers's soothing voice, the way he came home every day, took off his jacket, switched his shoes, buttoned his cardigan, and fed his fish. I didn't know Mr. Rogers was a psychologist. That those rituals were instilling me with a sense of object permanence. Even after the episode was over, I knew I'd turn on the TV the next day and there he would be, buttoning that darn cardigan once more. Doing the same thing again and again.

When my friend Mia died, it was one of those unexpected deaths that remind you of the fragility of the human body. Mia was my workout accountability buddy, so I saw her basically every weekday for two years. I happen to love those friends, the people from certain corners of life—your Starbucks friend, your Pilates friend, your work friend (Jennifer), your errand-running friend (also Jennifer), and your vacation friend (Jennifer again). These people pepper our lives with wisdom and the sustaining power of familiarity.

But Mia, my gym bestie, went into a diabetic coma. Right before she left this world, she was brain dead on a ventilator. It was shocking. The way she had been with me at the gym one day then on a ventilator in the hospital the next. The doctors had said her brain activity might return but everyone could tell by their tone it was hopeless. Then she was gone.

The first time I went to the gym after Mia died, I kept expecting to see her next to me. I remember programming my treadmill, thinking, *You can do this*. I half expected to see Mia next to me, half leaning on the armrests of the machine, telling me a meandering, overly detailed story about her daughter. I remember I did a half-hearted jog and barely broke a sweat. I felt lost. I tried to remember her, but for some reason, I could only picture Lady Aberlin, her luscious, thick eyelashes and her paisley muumuus billowing as she danced around the Neighborhood of Make-believe. Why couldn't I think of Mia, dancing in her car to "Hungry Like the Wolf" or "Girls Just Wanna Have Fun"? Waving her arms to all our favorite 1980s anthems.

On some level, faith, or the idea of it, is the cornerstone of just about everything we do on this planet. Faith is its own form of object permanence, like the spring following the long, cold winter. You need faith whether you're applying for a new job or going on a first date with that swiped-right Tinder hottie. After Mia died, I had to have faith that she'd found peace somewhere else. The problem was, after my father passed away, I'd stopped believing in an afterlife. A friend of mine who's a writer recently told me that ghosts are memories. Humans have energy. Energy can't be created or destroyed, only transformed. It just *is*. This is one way to look at it, but at the time, I remember wishing I could get a temporary pass to believing in heaven again, just for this one instance. I wanted so desperately to console myself with the idea that Mia had ended up somewhere other than the ground.

When my grandmother turned septic at ninety-four, I was the one to pull the plug. She'd made me her medical proxy because she knew her son, my biological father, wouldn't be able to do it. Her doctor told me he could give my grandmother some IV medication that would make her relatively better, but severely incapacitated, and she'd likely be in inpatient rehab for at least a year, if not the rest of her life. I had to make the call to let her go. I knew in my heart she wouldn't want to be in a nursing home. She'd told me this repeatedly all her life. She'd had a good run, but I still felt guilty about agreeing to palliative care.

I was with my grandmother when she died, holding her hand as she crossed over from this life to the next. I listened to her take her final, raspy breaths, otherwise known as the death rattle. She did not sweetly pass on. Witnessing the process of someone leaving their body was powerful and terrifying. When we come into the world our first breath is an inhalation and when we depart, our last breath is an exhalation, then there's nothing, just silence. An absence of spirit, an empty space for memory. I don't know where my grandmother went. All I know is she's still with me to this day, her indomitable spirit and humor, like Jennifer is always with me in spirit, stopping me from buying fake flower arrangements at Target or signs that say *Be the Energy You Want to Attract*.

Mia's death rocked me to my core. It felt like my own sister had died. Her daughter got married recently, and the whole time I was at her wedding, I kept thinking, *I can't believe Mia missed this. She would have loved it so much.* Mia lived for her kids. But did I seriously think my friend was up there, watching over us, with a halo around her head, or was this just a thing people said to ease their own sense of dread around death?

Sometime after Mia's daughter's wedding, I was at the gas station, filling up my tank. When I went inside the convenience store to buy a soda, I saw this supplement called kratom. A fellow patient at my rehab had been addicted to it. He was also a doctor and when he'd injured himself, he couldn't take pain pills because he was being drug tested for work. I knew kratom had a similar effect to opioids. I also knew it didn't show up on a drug test. I knew all these things.

Overwhelmed with anguish—or maybe it was just a moment of weakness, and I was looking for a reason to get high—I bought kratom and secretly took it for two weeks. The sad thing is it didn't even get me that high; by that point, I'd fried my neural pathways to the point where I could have taken quaaludes and still negotiated a settlement for a client then taught a kickboxing class on TikTok. Jennifer and Sam noticed my eyes looked unfocused. They presented me with a video they made of me nodding off during one of our podcasts.

At first, I felt defensive. I wondered why we were having another intervention when nothing all that serious was happening. But in the end, I admitted I was taking kratom. I'd been set up with a continuing-care plan when I left rehab. Part of that plan included random drug testing. But I'd chosen to relapse on kratom because I knew it wouldn't show up on a test. For those of you who don't know, this is classic addict behavior. A tragic event occurs, and our addict minds try to seduce us back to our former ways, even when those ways no longer serve us. After my relapse, I agreed to send the results to Jennifer as an extra layer of accountability. I couldn't run the risk of me relapsing again when there was so much at stake. Since then, I've learned to take it one day at a time. (Sometimes one breath at a time.) And I've been a hundred percent clean for over two years.

We can't prevent random tragic things from happening. We can't prevent our family members from getting terminal illnesses. We can't prevent drunk-driving accidents. But I could have chosen *not* to take kratom. I could have chosen to sit in my pain, which is its own memory, its own ghost. Its own Neighborhood of Make-believe. I could have honored my friend's death in all the ways it was cropping up, instead of running from the barbed sword of grief.

I think about Mia a lot these days. I think about how all these friends that get us through life are different manifestations of the best parts of ourselves. They remind us of who we really are. They remind us to love ourselves, even the supposedly unlovable, jiggly parts. They remind us to be better, to laugh harder.

Mia was so fun to be with at the gym. Sometimes, we would work out for real, her ponytail swishing as she talked about some TV show or our kids. She always told me I was gorgeous. I would take any excuse to stand with my feet off the belt of the treadmill and chug water or just look at the console, watching the illuminated seconds tick by. I didn't know then that time with Mia was precious, that I would never get those minutes back. I just wanted the time on the machine to run out so we could grab lunch or a smoothie. If I'd known, I would have set the timer on the treadmill to infinity and walked that existential belt to nowhere until they turned out the lights and told us to go home.

PICKLED

~~~~~~~~~

JEN

WHEN I GOT COVID in 2020, I was sick for months. I wandered into one room only to forget why I'd gone in there in the first place. My head felt like it was filled with Campbell's Cream of Mushroom Soup. I had to google actress + sex worker rom-com + movie to remember Julia Roberts's name. I thought I had dementia. I finally went to my doctor and told her all my symptoms: the headaches, the tingling in my arms, the long bouts of sleeping only to wake, exhausted and out of it. Even driving to her office resembled an odyssey worthy of Homer.

"I have constant headaches. I'm sleeping all the time, and I can't think clearly. I feel like hammered dog shit. I give this experience zero stars," I told my doctor, laughing, but it hurt to laugh, so I cried instead, the tears running down my cheeks, which also hurt.

It turned out I had long COVID. Weirdly, instead of prescribing an inhaler and a vitamin drip, my doctor recommended tennis. Or golf. Or an activity where I could use my brain and body simultaneously. Even though I was too weak to whip a gnat, I reluctantly acquiesced and left her office, skeptical but determined to get better. Josh and I loved watching tennis together; he'd played since he was a child. I started taking lessons. Sometimes, Josh would take me to the court and patiently toss balls for me to hit. He's still too good for us to play a match against each other, but he encouraged me to keep taking lessons and heaped praise on me as my forehand slowly improved.

At first, the brain fog lingered, and I doubted I'd return to my old self. Susan Sontag calls illness the "night-side" of life. I hoped my time there would be brief. When you don't feel well, sometimes it's like looking through a greasy window at other healthy people as they go about their business. I'm not neurotic but I had to stop myself from googling "long COVID" or going down rabbit holes on Reddit. I didn't want to attach myself to other people's timelines and symptomology.

Then I went on a mother–son trip to Seaside, Florida, with Roman and some of his friends and their moms, who I'd known for years because our kids were all the same age and had gone to preschool together. As a side bonus they all were very liberal and very anti-Trump, which had bonded us. One of the moms brought pickleball paddles and balls on that trip and so we played every day. I loved the game right away.

Pickleball was already in the zeitgeist at that point. The ball was light, like a wiffle ball, and the game was played in doubles. Though I started playing tennis, I ultimately found pickleball to be a skills equalizer. When I got back to OKC, I continued playing. I loved the sport, but more than that,

I loved the group. How could I not? Our group text was named "Get Rid of the Trumpers."

My obsession with pickleball coincided with the game bursting onto the national scene. Courts were popping up all over the city. I started playing pickleball after work as often as I could. Even if I was too damn tired or hungry and just wanted to go home and put on my sweatpants and watch a documentary about cults.

I happened to peep my close friend Tricia playing pickle-ball with a bunch of women while I was taking a tennis lesson. I invited her to play pickleball with my crew. From there, I met new friends and reacquainted myself with old friends. In the way that always happens when you share a common goal, passion, or hobby, I connected with new people at the courts and these new people have also become close friends. Most of my friends started playing around the same time I did and were all about the same skill level—aka zero skills—but I'd like to think we improved. We were all in the same season of our lives. We formed a bond through playing pickleball together on the regular. The companionship reminded me of smoking cigs and drinking wine on my porch with my girl-friends back in the day, only this situation was guilt-free and burned a lot more calories.

One of the picklers was an old friend, someone with whom I'd shared a lot of confidences about my husband over the years. She'd seen me at my absolute, codependent worst. A lot of the women were gay, which is neither here nor there, except that everyone was forward-thinking and progressive. I never hide my beliefs, but it was relaxing to be in an echo chamber. Tricia liked to remind me that we'd been to many happy hours together, but this was happy hour at its best because it didn't come with a hangover. I had to agree, although my previous hangovers didn't necessarily arrive with bruised elbows and shins.

I consider myself a somewhat competitive person. If you give me any kind of game, I will learn the rules and play to win with singular focus and steely determination. It's how I built my design business. It's how I turned our podcast from an idea to a solvent income stream. Competition got my dander up, and I thirsted to destroy my opponents. But I had no idea until I started playing pickleball just how competitive I truly was, not necessarily with other people but with myself. I took my playing seriously from the rip.

For me, pickleball was plain old satisfying, like eating a good meal, listening to Beethoven's Symphony No. 9, or watching the OKC Thunder make a buzzer-beater. I loved smacking the hell out of that ball and feeling the tension in the paddle. I loved watching the flight of the ball, filled with such intention, fighting to stay aloft. I felt its purpose in my body every time I stepped onto the court. And I felt my own purpose returning to me too—and that, more than anything, helped me reconnect my body to my mind again.

The hand-eye coordination required of racquet sports helped lift the fog of long COVID. More than that, tennis and pickleball centered me. My brain couldn't worry about politics or cogitate on work concerns when it was occupied with the mental calculations it had to make for my body to properly hit that yellow ball. The camaraderie of pickleball

comforted my soul. I began to feel like my old self again.
I had to stay focused and present, and if I smacked the ball
with enough power and grace, I could cut through the brain
fog and clear my mind of other anxieties. My relationship—
thwack—my children—*thwack*—the Republican Party—*thwack,*
thwack, thwack.

You might be operating under the assumption that you
aren't athletic enough to join a pickleball league. But I have
been absolutely destroyed by seventy-five-year-old women,
people in knee braces, and someone who had an asthma attack
on the court, called a time-out, took a few puffs on her inhaler, and then kept right on playing, like a boss. The good
news is that most people are so egotistical, so consumed with
their own insecurities and flaws that they don't have a hot
second to notice yours—or care about your so-called flaws
at all.

Pickleball isn't about how perfectly you play or even if you
win. Okay, it *is* about winning. But it's also about fostering
friendships with other picklers as well as yourself. It chal-
lenges assumptions and builds character.

I never thought I was too old to pick up a tennis racquet
or start playing pickleball. I refuse to buy into internalized
ageism. I exercise and use a little Botox to treat the exterior
manifestations of aging, but so far, I love getting older. I feel
more in shape since I quit smoking ten years ago than I did in
my thirties. More importantly, I like myself a whole lot more
than I ever did. Age allows the internal camera to see what
matters. It allows you to focus on the important things like
your health and spending time with the people you love, even

when they annoy you. I hope that whenever I do feel out of sorts, or have any regrets, I recall my bout with COVID, and what it felt like to be unable to think or to breathe. I hope that I can take a moment after a tough game to look up at the sky and feel grateful for what is instead of being morose about what isn't.

In October of 2022, Josh and I went to London together to see Roger Federer, who was retiring from tennis at the Laver Cup. There are few things Josh loves as much as Roger Federer: the kids, The Cure, candy, designer eyewear, and me on a good day. At the end of Federer's final doubles match, which he played with his longtime rival, Rafael Nadal (my favorite player), both Federer and Nadal started crying. Their keening was so loud, I could hear them in the stands, ten rows up. When I turned to Josh, to comment on the sheer volume and passion of their emotional display, I realized the sobbing I thought was emanating from these two iconic players on the court was actually coming from my husband. Josh was absolutely bawling; I'm talking Niagara Falls levels of tears and snot.

A lump formed in my throat. Josh has always been unabashed about showing his emotion. His vulnerability was one of the things that drew me to him all those years ago. He wasn't afraid to reveal his tender heart. He never had to be "the tough guy." Squeezing his hand, I realized that all of the shit sandwiches of our early days might just pay off in our empty-nest days. We both love traveling, tennis, and most of all, our children, and each other. Seeing Josh ugly-cry for

Roger Federer reminded me how much I love him. The real him. Blood, snot, and tears. It reminded me that we've always been a team, even when I thought we weren't.

I can't say that racquet sports turned me back into the person I was before the pandemic. Do we ever go back to what we once were? All I know is, moving my body around on those courts, I started to regenerate—physically, mentally, even spiritually. I felt myself healing every day as I ran myself ragged, and I loved every minute of it. It reminded me of something high school and college athletes know well: Even if you struggle to return a serve, there's nothing better than showing up and leaving it all on the court, for the team and for yourself.

HOME SWEET HOME

ANGIE

WHEN I WAS A girl, I was convinced I would marry Blake Carrington on *Dynasty*, a show I was technically not supposed to watch but did anyway. Maybe it's an indication of my daddy issues, but I'd sit in front of our TV, mesmerized by Blake's erudite accent and fancy-schmancy mansion, the way the entire Carrington family would come down to family dinner in evening wear like they were going to the Oscars. I thought Krystle was the most elegant woman I'd ever seen—a beautiful, busty, blonde, blue-eyed secretary who married an oil baron and had the massive shoulder pads to prove it. Of course, I was devastated when Pamela Sue Martin, the actress playing Fallon Carrington, left the show—her character's car was hit by a truck—but primetime soaps being what they were, an amnesiac Fallon magically reappeared in the next season played by Emma Samms (who looked and sounded nothing like Pamela Sue Martin).

But watching TV and *being* on TV are two totally different things, as are "scripted" versus "non-scripted," though non-scripted doesn't mean there's no plan or storyboard. When I found myself on a reality TV show, I was thrilled at first. All those fantasies of my girlhood watching *Dynasty* came flooding back to me, the silly, predictable plots that either ended on cliffhanger or all resolved so neatly. The cat-fighting in swimming pools while hotels burned. Joan Collins in general. Her wigs and glamorous outfits. I would shut off the TV and pretend to be doing my homework as soon as I heard my parents' footsteps in the hall, but I wondered if my life would ever be as exciting.

When I was shooting *Sweet Home Oklahoma*, the "set" was my house or Jennifer's house, or some restaurant we'd frequented so often it was like an extension of our actual homes. It was surreal to have cameras and boom operators be in places that were so personal and familiar, but it was also strange how quickly I adjusted to thirty people using my downstairs powder room or smoking on the same back porch, where I'd once smoked countless cigarettes, worrying about my future.

Fame never held any luster for me. I never wanted to be an actress or a rock star. When I was a kid, the closest Gen X ever got to reality TV was *Candid Camera*. Did Bethenny Frankel grow up saying, "When I'm an adult, I want to record my minor and major life events for all the world to pick apart like a starving buzzard? I want to sit on Instagram talking about moisturizer and chicken salad?" No. But as a fellow tightwad when it came to spending money on myself,

I do adore her drugstore serum recs. My point is that when Jennifer approached me about doing *Sweet Home Oklahoma*, I couldn't say no. Kirk had drained our bank account to feed his rampant sex addiction. I was broke and desperately needed the extra income. The casting agency approached Jennifer and she told them that I'd be perfect for the show. I don't know what I did, but it must have been good because they met me and agreed after one conversation.

The only teensy-weensy glitch to this otherwise perfect setup: I was high on pills for the entire run of *Sweet Home Oklahoma*. Since it was before I went to rehab and got clean, I was too detached to participate fully in the experience. The editors had to cut away from me during night shoots because I was so zonked out on a combination of Percs and morphine that sometimes I would nod out or fall asleep on set.

Forget the being-on-TV part; it turns out that the "reality" of reality was too much for me. Of course, Jennifer worked overtime to shield my little naps from the producers and the viewers. I later learned how stressful that was for her.

That said, there were parts I enjoyed. The people we worked with were wonderful and kind and it was a blast to go to work with Jennifer. There was something soothing about someone else providing the itinerary for my life. Every day, the producers said, saying, "Okay, Angie, now you're going to this restaurant," or, "Now you'll go to early morning basketball practice." Being on *Sweet Home* was like writing "make bed" on a to-do list so I could cross it off at the end of the day. No matter what funny scene ended up on the cutting room floor, it was a strange experience to film yourself living and think about strangers subsequently watching it while they ate takeout.

There's something magical about being the viewer of your life, rather than the agent of it. A passenger along for the ride if not a participant in the story. My parents said go to church, and I went. They said participate in purity culture and I participated. Sometimes, on set, I thought of those stolen moments in front of my parents' television, the way the Carringtons and the Colbys performed their own ritualistic TV dance, a paean to deep 1980s capitalism. The way the Evangelical Church had carved its own reality, its own set of rules. Soon I would be following the steps and traditions of a twelve-step program, but I didn't know it yet. I still hadn't found my personal blueprint, the one that would involve AA, being single, and recording *I've Had It* with Jennifer.

On the podcast, Jen and I have a hundred percent control of the narrative. What we say and do is totally organic. I cogently express my own views and I like what I have to say. Reality television wasn't necessarily the opposite; I was still myself, but the producers edited it however the heck they wanted. Again, Jennifer and I were very clear that we didn't want to be edited to seem like we were in conflict when we weren't, but still, we didn't have control over the end product. It was our *lives*, but it wasn't our show. Regardless, the controlled chaos provided an escape. There I was on TV, in my cozy red bathrobe, the robe I still wear, without any makeup, looking like shit on a shingle, which is seemingly brave and vulnerable—just ask Pamela Anderson—but it wasn't an honest portrayal of who I really was. I was still hiding from myself. It took me a long time to wake up. Almost like I had amnesia. But instead of a British actress, wandering in from the set of another soap opera to play me, I had to be myself. My real, honest-to-goodness, no-holds-barred, nothing-on-the-cutting-room-floor self.

When Jennifer and I were still doing *Sweet Home Oklahoma*, we received tons of letters and messages from viewers who were addicts or whose spouses or kids were struggling. They talked about how inspiring it was to see Jennifer and Josh speak so openly about their marital problems. My one regret (or maybe my ten thousandth) is that I wasn't more of my authentic self with Jennifer and our fans the whole time. I wish I had stood in my red robe and admitted how badly I needed help. I wish I'd asked Jennifer to lead me home, sweet home, where I always belonged.

THE REDEMPTION TOUR

~~~~~~~~~~

JEN

ONE RAINY SATURDAY, I sat at the dining room table looking at the designs for a client's new primary en suite. I heard Josh's car pull into the driveway and he came inside and grabbed a sparkling water out of the fridge. I could tell by his facial expression there was something he wanted to tell me but couldn't, so I braced for whatever came next.

When you're with an addict, everything revolves around them, their mood, the general tone of their day. They co-opt the vibe, not necessarily on purpose, but more out of a sense of wanting you to see how well they're doing. Their sobriety and their AA meeting become conversational mainstays. Josh was no different. He started rambling about his therapy session with Dr. K. I glanced at my blueprints on the table, drawn to my own work.

"Dr. K. wants me to start doing ketamine therapy," Josh said.

"Fuck you," I said, horrified. "Fuck Dr. K. If that mother-fucker wants you to take drugs, you're both fucking insane." My hand shook as I took a sip of my water.

"Okay, no problem," he said, then left the room to go upstairs and lie down.

He never mentioned the ketamine therapy again and neither did I. But the idea of it hovered menacingly around the house. About a month later, I happened to be watching *60 Minutes*. Anderson Cooper was doing a segment on psychedelic medicine: for nearly two decades, researchers at Johns Hopkins had been giving psilocybin to test subjects who struggled with addiction and depression. I sat right up and cranked the volume. To me, the idea of taking drugs to treat a drug addiction sounded dangerous and irresponsible; we'd been touted abstinence-only recovery. I felt my blood pressure increase and had to do four-part breathing as I reached for my laptop. After a serious investigation, I walked right into the bedroom where Josh was looking at some photos and said, "I think I owe you an apology."

Josh quit SSRIs in 2020 to start doing controlled ketamine therapy under the supervision of a doctor in a medical setting. Right away, I saw a significant change in him, more than I'd ever seen with any prescriptive medication. I'm not suggesting that SSRIs don't work or advocating that anyone should stop or start any protocol without consulting their psychopharmacologist or medical doctor. I'm just saying psych meds are a billion-dollar industry and that this industry slaps pills on every problem from sleeplessness to hair loss. Also, if you don't look underneath that rock when you're taking your little pills, you're just painting over the problem, which leads to—you guessed it—more pills.

Controlled ketamine therapy opened the floodgates. Josh started crying more often than usual. A young mom would walk into our neighborhood sushi restaurant with a baby, and Josh would just begin weeping like he was in perimenopause. Dylan and Roman often joked about it, the way Josh cried at TV shows or puppies in commercials. But Josh kept trotting off to the clinic to get his intravenous ketamine treatment. He put on earphones and listened to indie or alternative music, anything that soothed his inner demons. He told me that whenever he felt afraid, he built a room with me, Roman, and Dylan in it. The room smelled like chocolate chip cookies. If he encountered any of the trauma of his past, any monsters or anything scary, he knew he could return to that room, to our love. He saw again and again how his love for me, and our family, outlived his childhood fears of abandonment.

What saved Josh, in the end, was connecting to that part of himself that knew and generated love, not just self-love, but our love for him. It was a lesson I needed to learn too, that love can conquer fear, and weirdly my former addict–alcoholic husband had to take drugs (in a controlled setting) to figure that out.

Life can be untenable even for the strongest among us, but for addicts, keeping your family and career afloat can feel like trying to sail a dinghy through a squall, one brutal wave after another. After a scandal rocked his law firm, Josh voluntarily resigned his license and remained in self-imposed exile for twelve years. But during his whole renaissance of self, he decided he was ready to reapply for his bar license, which terrified me, although I knew the day would eventually arrive. Oklahoma City is a small town and the story of what happened became typical fodder for small-minded gossip. Josh stopped practicing law for years to pursue photography, something for which he has an affinity, though it never held his heart and mind the way practicing law did.

As soon as Josh decided he was ready, we met with an attorney who specialized in helping physicians who'd lost their medical licenses. Josh wasn't a doctor, but to reapply for a bar license, he had to go through a yearlong reinstatement process. He had to spell out what he did, why he did it, what happened after that, and who he was now. He had to call character witnesses. The DA and the Bar Association were like the KGB, FBI, and CIA rolled into one eavesdropping organization. They looked at every facet of his life. They wanted his medical records. They wanted his driving record. They wanted his credit report. It was massive. The two of us discussed whether this whole thing was even worth it. What if he got rejected and the rejection triggered a relapse? No matter how often all the attorneys, his addictionologist, and Dr. K. told Josh he'd punished himself far more than the system ever would or should have, we worried.

Newly sober Angie immediately agreed to testify. Sober Pumps was a witness for Sober Josh. Another close friend in recovery was a character witness. I was a witness. An extended family member in recovery was a witness. A former federal judge and close family friend was a witness. Even the district attorney was a witness. The Bar Association typically took an adversarial position with attorneys, but in Josh's case, they didn't. Josh had always been honest with them regarding his addiction struggles and other shortcomings. And that redeemed him.

When the day of the hearing came, I had to lift the damn rock yet again. I had to dredge up a lot of our past pain points, which is exactly what I never wanted to do again. I thought or I hoped that I had left it all behind me. But there it was again: our story in all its sadness and joy. The long nights crying alone, and the belly laughs together. Josh was (and is) a dedicated, empathetic lawyer. His impetus for being an attorney has always been to help people. Before he resigned, he'd helped so many clients get out of jail and so many friends get sober. We weren't ashamed about our experiences with addiction, so we were a resource for a lot of friends and neighbors. I testified about all of that.

A committee voted on Josh's reinstatement. Then the decision went to the Oklahoma Supreme Court. For the next six months, we waited . . . and waited. Josh tried to act casual, but I could tell he was a complete and utter wreck. I was an even bigger wreck but I tried to pretend I had it all together. In October 2023, I was in my office, sitting at my desk, when Josh walked in, bawling.

"I got reinstated," he said simply. "The court voted unanimously to reinstate me."

I started crying and we embraced. That unrecognizable feeling of joy, after everything—it was like we'd crossed our own personal Rubicon. I want to say it made us whole again, but the truth is we were never whole to start with. We were a perpetual work in progress, trying to find our footing.

I cried for a solid thirty minutes that day. I cried for the twenty-seven-year-old version of myself at Flip's Wine Bar. I cried for the emotional pain I endured during my pregnancies, worrying that Josh wouldn't stay sober long enough to be a father. I cried for my mother, who never self-actualized. I cried for my father and all he endured in Vietnam and never talked about. I cried for Pumps, who was finally sober after being addicted to opioids for a decade. I cried for my sons, who had become such successful, kind, intelligent, wonderful grown-ups, despite their parents' problems. I'm not kidding myself. I'm sure they're going to have thousands of dollars' worth of therapy at some point in the near or distant future. I'm aware that Josh and I likely passed some of our dysfunction onto our kids. But it says a lot that both young men want to go to law school like their dad. They see the good in their father, even when he couldn't.

Josh is light-years away from the person he was in 2007. He worked so hard to get sober, and he works diligently every day to maintain his sobriety by helping other people maintain their sobriety. Nothing is more important to him because he knows everything is on the line. He's been in recovery for over a decade. He's a committed attorney who puts his clients' needs before his own. He's also one of our most popular guests on the podcast. He supported my endeavor to write this book and thought it was worth it for me to be totally honest about every aspect of our story, even if it didn't always paint him in the best light. That's the kind of man he is. If he thinks his story will benefit even a single person, he wants it to be told.

Right after Josh got reinstated, we were all on vacation in Capri. It was a perfect day, one of those bright summer afternoons, and we were on a boat. I looked up at the birds diving off the cliffs into the rippling navy water. They were so graceful, doing exactly what nature intended. The whole scene summoned a presence of mind I hadn't experienced in years. There we were, the birds, my sons, and Josh and I, all connected to this beautiful place, where people were born and died in wealth and poverty, in good times and bad—and I thought, *Yes, serenity and peace.* When I look at Josh now, I see the man I vowed to be with in sickness and in health. And isn't a vow a sacred oath you swear to uphold? That's what we did, Josh and I. That's who we are. That's what we built, together, forever. A marriage. I wouldn't trade it for any kind of normal.

GRIEF IS A MOTHER

JEN

ONE FRIDAY EVENING IN early July, Josh and I were at a wedding in Montana. It was one of those enchanted weekends when everything felt magical; the kind of weekend when you glance up from your tennis game to see bald eagles swooping over lush, emerald-green valleys, and it's so beautiful you almost start to believe in America again. I remember thinking, *Josh is sober and in a good space. Angie's sober. The podcast is monetizing. Dylan's graduating from Syracuse and applying to law school. Roman is applying to colleges. I did it. I raised the kids. I saved my marriage.*

Sitting at dinner with some friends, I felt like I could finally exhale. Then I looked down at my iPhone and saw Roman's name flashing across the screen.

I felt my body girding itself in anticipation. We'd just Face-Timed a couple of hours earlier. I knew my son would have texted me if he had a benign question, so the fact that he was calling meant that something terrible had happened.

"I have to take this," I said, rising from the table. Josh looked at me. My voice must have indicated alarm. "It's Roman," I added. My husband followed me as I answered the call, wending my way through the tables of happy diners whose lives would likely continue as before. They would likely chew their steaks, split their molten chocolate lava cakes, and drive home to pay their babysitters.

"Roman?" I said. But all I could hear was indescribable wailing. "Mom," he finally managed to say. "Zach drowned."

"What?" I said, as though if I hadn't heard him, maybe it wouldn't be true. Maybe if I hadn't heard those words spoken in that exact order, Zach would still be alive and standing on the dock and my son wouldn't be keening into my eardrum when I was so far away from him.

When Roman was born, I imagined his whole life stretching out before him. Holding him on my chest, I saw him as a cute toddler in diapers, then dressed as Spider-Man for Halloween, then in high school, playing basketball. I saw him applauding as he threw his cap in the air at college graduation, walking him down the aisle at his wedding. Attending his graduation from law school. Holding his baby in my arms. Him clutching my hand as I took my last breath. Here's what I didn't imagine, and what any parent never imagines for their child: a freak accident, a tragic drowning at Grand Lake.

The evening Roman found out his childhood friend died, he'd been sitting in his room when his phone started blowing up. The group text grew increasingly disjointed and frantic as the terrible picture emerged like an image from a Polaroid. Zach had just received a D1 scholarship to play football at

Dartmouth and now he was no longer alive. Every feeling flooded Roman's mind: disbelief, inconsolable pain, terror, horror, shock. I asked him, "Are you sure?" Something about someone dying so young is so unfathomable, I found myself asking question after question to stave off the tragic reality. Roman told me later that, sitting in his bedroom, texting with people he'd known since he was a little boy, he felt like his childhood ended in the blink of an eye.

Josh and I immediately left the restaurant and went to the hotel to frantically search for flights home to OKC. I was in get-back-to-my-child mode. We flew to Oklahoma on the first flight out the next day. If I could have, I would have beamed myself to my son's side the second I heard. Being away from Roman when he heard this news, knowing he was in such pain, was beyond difficult. Roman's older brother, Dylan, was home from Syracuse, and we sent Javi, a young man who worked at my office and who knew Roman very well, to go and check up on them, so we knew Roman wasn't alone. All Josh and I could do was cry and hold each other as we shared our disbelief and overwhelming sadness for sweet Zach and his family. I knew full well that grief was a long haul and recovery was jagged. It wasn't a straight shot from point A to point B. I knew that the subsequent phases could be just as difficult, the ones after the funeral when everyone went back to their everyday lives.

Every time I thought of that child's parents, my breath would catch in my throat. I'd taken so much for granted. Maybe my problems had been normal-people problems all along.

Several weeks later, Roman's school year started. He seemed to be turning a corner or at least going through the motions. He was studying for his ACT, writing his college essays, and hanging out with friends. Life was continuing apace. I hoped that he would be able to find happiness his senior year of high school, and worried that he wouldn't. The sadness came in unexpected, intolerable waves. But we found ourselves sharing funny memories of Zach, like the time I took the kids to Braum's for burgers and shakes when they were still in middle school. Zach had recently had a growth spurt and was already six feet tall. When I asked the kids what they wanted to eat, Roman asked for a junior cheeseburger, and Zach turned to me and said, "Mrs. Welch, I'll take a bag of burgers, please."

Roman and I glanced at each other. The "bag of burgers" at Braum's contained five sizable cheeseburgers and was likely a meal for an entire family. Zach ate all five burgers. We still laugh remembering that.

One rainy Saturday, Angie and I got a call from Kamala Harris's campaign that they wanted us to go to Washington, DC, and interview Kamala's husband, Doug Emhoff. Pumps and I started prepping. The next day, I was packing for my afternoon flight to DC and hanging out with Josh in our walk-in closet, curating my outfit. I remember I held up a few skirt options and said, "Should I wear this or this? These shoes or these shoes?"

Josh was pointing at a pencil skirt when the doorbell went off. Tubby and Cha Cha went wild. Josh was naked because he was about to hop in the shower, so I went to see who was at the door.

An older gentleman I vaguely recognized stood on the stoop.

"I don't know if you remember me," he said, "but I'm Javi's grandfather."

I immediately disassociated. I knew it wasn't good if this man was at my door. He looked at me, his eyes full of something I couldn't describe.

"Javi's been shot," he said finally. "They killed him."

"Are you sure?" I said. The news was too terrible to comprehend, and I needed two to three more seconds so I could brace for impact. I kept thinking, *Maybe he's wrong, and there's some other explanation. Maybe no one can find Javi and he's at another hospital as a John Doe.* I felt numb and tingly like some other force was in control of my body.

Josh came to the front door with a robe wrapped around him and immediately started crying. "Did I hear that right? Did I just hear that right?" he asked.

Javi's grandfather came in and told us the whole story, how Javi had been held up at gunpoint in a parking lot and then shot. He was only twenty-four years old.

I know there's a standard hagiography that accompanies the dead and the dying, but Javi was the kindest, most selfless person I've ever known. The kind of person we should all aspire to be. He took care of his three little brothers. He went to his grandparents' house every Sunday to make sure their trash was taken out. But unlike most people on the planet, he never complained about having to do these mundane tasks or told anybody about them. He never needed credit or praise. He never made anything about himself.

When the FedEx guy came by my office recently, he asked me, "Where's Javi been?" After I told him what happened, he got tears in his eyes and said, "That kid was so nice. He would come out and help me unload boxes and help me deliver them to other places." I never knew Javi did that. He just quietly did the right thing.

This chapter is not going to be a screed against gun violence, because I know that we all agree about that. Nor is it about how truly terrible it is when a young person suddenly and senselessly dies. But Javi's death shattered everyone who knew him in places we didn't think could be shattered. In the aftermath of Javi's passing, it would occur to me how unfair it was that Mama Worth got to live until she was in her nineties, yet she caused all sorts of trouble at her nursing home before she died, embroiling herself and other folk in nasty gossip. Why did she get to live for so long while Javi had to die? Why did fate have to be so cruel?

I pulled up to my office the Monday after Javi died, and I could only stay in that building for ten minutes. It was too painful. When I returned later with Angie, I idled by the front doors. I just sat there in my car, clutching the steering wheel. Pumps put her hand on my shoulder. I looked at the planter by the entrance. It held a big healthy plant with waxy, tropical green leaves. I recalled how only a year ago, that plant was shriveled and near death. I told Javi we needed to call it.

"Let's just go to the garden center and get a new plant," I said.

"No, J. Dub," Javi said. "I've been researching on YouTube, and I've diagnosed the plant with this disease. I've watched a video on how I can cure it, and I think I can treat it and bring it back."

It looked like a lost cause to me, but he seemed so heartfelt about it that I told him to give it a whirl. Javi meticulously treated, sprayed, and scrubbed each leaf every Friday for the next year. I noticed the plant had improved, but I don't remember if we ever discussed it. Why didn't I say anything about it or compliment Javi on his green thumb? Why didn't I tell him what a great job he'd done repotting and resuscitating that plant?

On that Monday after Javi died, sitting in my car with Pumps, I noticed that the plant was four times its previous size. It was big, full, vibrant, and alive. When Javi died, a part of me did too. The young man who Cha Cha thought was her soulmate, who thought Jolly Ranchers were a food group and drank Powerade like it was water, who cannonballed into hotel swimming pools, who loved sports podcasts and humored me about my true-crime podcasts, who had helped Roman through his pain at the loss of his friend, that man was gone, and our lives would never be the same. I would never be the same.

Recently, Roman's basketball coach told him grief never disappears; it just reorganizes itself. Maybe this is what life is: a constant reorganization and dilation of emotions and events. The lazy Susan spins without ever hinting at what's to come. But we know, don't we? We get a hint of it every time a baby is born and every time someone we love tragically and inexplicably dies. The wheel spins, the sun rises, and we remember.

Even though I'm not a plant person, I vowed to myself that I'd keep that thing alive. I knew Javi would say: "J. Dub, you're sad now, but you'll be okay. You've got to take care of this plant. You've got to take care of your business, and you've got to take care of those dogs. Take care of Tubby and Cha Cha and Josh and Roman and Dylan."

I grabbed Javi's water can and gave his plant a drink.

CONCLUSION: LAST NIGHT, A PODCAST SAVED MY LIFE

ANGIE

THE OTHER WEEK, JEN and I were sitting around, preparing for our podcast with Kamala Harris. In 2020, we had watched in wonder as she stood in her sneakers with her phone pressed to her ear, saying, "We did it, Joe." I remember the collective breath of relief watching those election results. To say Jennifer and I despise Trump doesn't begin to cover it. We live in a purple city in a red state; yet we remain baffled by what happened in 2016 and shocked, appalled, saddened, and terrified by the election results in 2024. But maybe we aren't. Maybe this is America. Maybe the backassward thinking of the right is more backassward than we ever knew or understood. Sometimes, the backassward-ness terrifies me so much that I pull my car over to talk myself off a cliff. On November 6, 2024, I couldn't stop crying. I couldn't eat. I had to take beta-blockers to slow my heart rate down so that I could manage to choke down a banana.

This is all to say that America needs a time-out. Desperately. Not tomorrow, but now. Today. How about an America that isn't completely divided and fucked-up beyond repair? An America where women aren't defending their reproductive rights every second?

I used to give my kids time-outs when they misbehaved, but if they cried, I would buckle. America doesn't need that kind of a time-out. They need the kind of time-out my parents doled out to me and my siblings when we were kids. If I ever talked back, I would get sent to my room without supper. I would have privileges taken away and extra household chores heaped onto my already substantial list.

But back to Kamala Harris. If you'd told Jennifer and me that we would be in our nation's capital one day, asking Harris what she'd had it with, and that she'd be extremely kind, funny, and personable, or that we'd one day interview Bernie Sanders or Gavin Newsom, or sit down to play "Had It or Hit It" with Barack Obama, I would have told you to shut the front door.

When we started the podcast, we didn't know where it would take us or how successful it would be. I considered it a lark. I thought the worst thing that could happen was we'd lose some money on the recording equipment. I just knew I wanted to work with Jennifer as often as possible.

We both enjoyed filming *Sweet Home Oklahoma* but had surrendered control of the final, finished product to the whim of the editors in post-production. I never knew which scenes or takes would ultimately end up in the show. On *I've Had It*, we pick the guests. We don't edit, but we listen to the tape. For the first time in my life, I feel like I have my own authentic voice and I like how I sound—funny, sometimes ridiculous, but forceful, and opinionated. I show up as my full self to that podcast studio; if I'm annoyed, I use it. When I clap the show on in the intro, I feel like it brings me into the room. I leave my problems at the door.

Jennifer and I have always been able to converse freely and to make each other laugh, but then something else happened. I wouldn't say we've become political pundits, but we've filled a void the political podcast landscape never knew it had—middle-aged, liberal, Democrat, cis-het, white women who live in a red state. After Kamala Harris replaced Biden as the Democratic nominee, we began investing more time and energy into our news segments, and we picked up more and more subscribers. By the time we went to the DNC and got to interview Barack Obama, the podcast no longer felt like a lark.

I never thought *I've Had It* would take off or gather the kind of momentum it did. I never envisioned any kind of real success or happiness for myself. I didn't think we would write this book (or that I would be sitting here, in my red robe, typing the conclusion). I didn't think we would get such a loyal, wonderful group of followers and fans. Every time we do a live show, and I meet some of our listeners, and they tell us the positive effect we've had on their lives, I feel, on some level, like I'm talking to my close friends or my kids' friends. When queer young people who grew up in small towns in Texas or Tennessee tell me how they wished that Jennifer or I were their moms, that is not a statement I take lightly. I know I speak for Jennifer when I say we feel beyond honored to hear that. Jennifer and I will continue to fight for LGBTQIA+ rights and for people of color every single day.

In the AA community, they talk a lot about writing gratitude lists. Anyone who knows me, knows I am bad about doing that kind of stuff. But if I were to write a gratitude list, one of the first things I would say is I am grateful for this community. The podcast has given me more than I have given it. It's cliché but it's true that you always receive more than you give. I'm grateful for this podcast. I'm grateful for our listeners and for y'all, the fans. I'm grateful for the server who heats up my queso until it's PIPING HOT. I'm grateful for our producer, the resident tech genius responsible for editing *I've Had It* and running my Instagram. I'm grateful for my kids, who are all brilliant geniuses and future Nobel Laureates in their own right. I'm grateful Emily rushed Kappa Kappa Gamma. I'm grateful for Jennifer Welch. She saved my life. But really, when it comes right down to it, when I take off my makeup at night and look at myself in the mirror, I am grateful for my own damn resilience and ability to stay sober, one day at a time, no matter what happens.

Having a podcast takes more preparation, research, and reading than I would have thought. Sometimes, juggling *I've Had It* with my day job is overwhelming, but to be honest, Jennifer drives a lot of what goes on behind the scenes. She'll call me and say, "I think we should have the White House Press Secretary Karine Jean-Pierre as a guest," or, "What about Cody Rigsby?" If I'm not familiar with the guests, I do my own internet sleuthing or read up about them, though in the case of Cody Rigsby, no Peloton bikes were harmed in the recording of this podcast. After learning everything I can, so that I feel I can speak intelligently, I try to prepare insightful questions, though usually all our guests are so thoughtful and funny, they do most of the work for us. We should all be as accomplished as Karine Jean-Pierre! Some of my absolute dream guests would be Rachel Maddow, Anderson Cooper, and Oprah. Rachel, if you're reading this, please call me!

Some shows are better than others. So are some days. Some days you interview Barack Obama at the DNC. Some days you celebrate your kid graduating from college and others you have to pull the plug on your grandmother or watch your friend die. Some days you have hope that your ex-husband will keep it together and other days that feels like a far-flung possibility. My greatest hope for Kirk is that he stays healthy, because that is what's best for my children. The thing about being young is you think you're so old. And the thing about being older is that you wish you could be young again, only with the wisdom of being older. You think, *I am so wise. I have lived through it all. What else could possibly happen?* I happen to know I am not wise. All I know is anything could happen at any time, and if it does, I hope I know what to do.

Wait. Did I mention we interviewed Barack Obama? When we were flying from OKC to Chicago O'Hare, all I could think was, *I hope I don't sound like a total idiot or start crying the second I see him.* I worried that all the outfits I brought would be terrible. Why did I buy all my clothes on sale at Amazon? Why didn't I buy fancy, designer clothes like Jennifer, who always looks so chic? Then, as the plane touched down in the Midwest, I remembered something my mother always said which had to do with how to be a polite house-guest but applied to this situation. Her advice was basically no matter what, say thank you. If you feel shy or don't like the food, if you're in someone else's house, just say thank you.

To be honest, that whole DNC week was like a dream. We spoke with Stacey Abrams. We heard Michelle Obama speak. Oprah. (I was in the same room as Oprah.) It was electric. And did I mention we met Barack Obama? We were filled with such hope. Jennifer even waved an American flag. True, our hopes were summarily dashed when a certain person got elected. If there's one thing I've learned, it's that you have to keep fighting, even when victory seems remote or impossible.

I don't know what the future has in store for the country. I remember my grandmother talking about World War II, how reading the names of the young men who died every day in the newspaper was the worst time. I worry we are sliding in that direction. Everything feels like a Will Smith movie about the end of the world. It worries me and sometimes it's hard to find an objective, fact-checked news source. That's why Jennifer and I are driven to work so hard on our podcast and on *IHIP News*. We want to be a source of humor *and* truth.

The reason Jennifer and I banter so well is that we've been through a lot together. We have an Olympic-sized pool of combined tears, but there's also been a lot of laughter. A lot of Greek salads with extremely good salad dressing. A whole bunch of queso. We've traded in Jen's porch for the podcast studio these days, and we've both quit smoking, but it's basically the same idea: we talk through everything, even the scary stuff. I try to be honest with myself and to keep the lights on, even when I don't want to. I call my sponsor when I feel bad, or I call Jennifer. I call someone who will listen to me without judgment.

To our wonderful kind, funny, smart, compassionate listeners and all the people we've met in line at live podcasts in Nashville, Atlanta, Los Angeles, San Francisco, Boston, Seattle, and Brooklyn. To all the patriots, gaytriots, and theytriots, we hear you. We see you. We love you. We will fight and vote for your rights until we have no fight left and even then, we will keep fighting. I will have my grandchildren who haven't been born yet roll my tired, wrinkly ass to the voting booth.

I leave y'all with this: A new friend of mine recently told me about the Net of Indra, a Hindu myth about a giant gill net that stretches across the entire universe. At every intersection of rope sits a gem, reflecting the one next to it, and the one next to it, and the one next to it, onto infinity. It's a beautiful image about connection, even when we feel very far from one another or from ourselves. In a sense, this is how I view the world—that we are each distinct yet connected.

Finally, I no longer take beta-blockers when we do live podcasts. Okay, I still feel nervous AF, but I don't feel like I'm going to have a myocardial infarction and die on the spot as soon as I hear our producer say, "Put your hands together for Jennifer Welch and Angie "Pumps" Sullivan!"

After Jennifer and I came back to our hotel room keyed up

from being at the DNC (where we'd just met Obama), and we took off our makeup, put on moisturizer, and got into our beds, it was hard to go to sleep. We chatted briefly, lying there in the dark, like Bert and Ernie. As usual, Jennifer fell asleep before I did. Listening to her soft breathing, the white noise of the air conditioner barely masking the thrum of the freeway, my heart full to bursting, I looked over at my sleeping best friend and whispered, "We did it, Jen."